PLATE I

LADY IN PROMENADE COSTUME

After Desrais. From the " Galerie des Modes." 1776

MODES & MANNERS
ORNAMENTS

LACE FANS GLOVES WALKING-
STICKS PARASOLS JEWELRY
AND TRINKETS

BY

MAX VON BOEHN

TRANSLATED FROM THE GERMAN

*With 241 illustrations in
monochrome and 16 in colour*

LONDON & TORONTO
J. M. DENT & SONS LTD.
NEW YORK: E. P. DUTTON & CO. INC.

FIRST PUBLISHED IN ENGLAND . 1929

345696

PRINTED IN GREAT BRITAIN

PREFACE

As its title implies, this book tells the story of those highly important "trifles" which have from the first accompanied the progress of Fashion as characteristic attributes. An antique snuff-box, a pair of gloves, or a needle-case are no less eloquent than a gown or costume, as their wearers and owners rise before our mind's eye and tell us of a bygone age. Forgotten tales of joy and sorrow leap into life, and many an historic figure first becomes for us a living person when anecdote links his name with a walking-stick or a watch. In this way an enchanting region of social history is unrolled before our eyes. We may stroll beneath the parasols of the ancient Egyptians, watch a Grecian beauty gracefully fanning herself, and may thence make our way through the centuries until, half-blinded by the pearl- and diamond-encrusted splendours of the court of *le Roi soleil*, we find grateful relief in the homelier light of the days when "gold was given for iron." [1]

Planned as a supplement to our series on Modes and Manners, this little book is assured of a welcome from all lovers of that series, besides being well qualified to win new friends for this cultural history in miniature. As in the *Modes* series, the text is here enriched with very numerous and excellent illustrations, the material for which we owe to the kind assistance of the National Museum and the Cabinet of Drawings and Engravings in Munich. Special thanks are also due to Herr Professor Glaser, director of the National Art Library, Berlin, who kindly placed a wealth of material at our disposal.

F. Bruckmann A.-G., publishers,
Munich, Autumn, 1928.

[1] In the War of Liberation against Napoleon the German people voluntarily brought articles of gold to the Treasury to be melted down, women even offering their wedding rings and receiving iron rings in return.

v

ACKNOWLEDGMENTS

THE Publishers' thanks are due to Lady Ryan for permission to reproduce the illustrations on pages 81 and 85 from *Royal and Historical Gloves*, by W. B. Redfern; to the Victoria and Albert Museum for the illustration on page 76; to the Ashmolean Museum, Oxford, for the illustrations on pages 77 and 93; and to the Saffron Walden Museum for that on page 77; and to Messrs. Methuen & Co. Ltd. for their kind co-operation.

CONTENTS

vii

ILLUSTRATIONS IN COLOUR

ILLUSTRATIONS IN HALF-TONE

xii

xiv

Rubens   JACQUELINE DE CAESTRE   *Brussels*

CHAPTER I

LACE

LACE appears very late in the long history of needle-craft. The ancients, it is true, produced thinly or loosely woven fabrics and employed various forms of open-work, but lace was unknown to them. In the Middle Ages, the energies of women were restricted within the household and were thus to all intents and purposes forced into the channels of artistic hand-work. At that period women excelled in all kinds of embroidery and produced something closely akin to lace in netting, or *lacis*, yet it was not till the second half of the sixteenth century that true lace appeared. Its forerunners can, of course, be traced back over a long period. The art of open work in linen material by such methods as drawing out threads from the body of the fabric (drawn thread-work cutting out threads (cut-work), or bunching threads together without cutting or withdrawal, can be traced to ancient Egypt was known to later antiquity, and examples of it have been found in Peru.

Pictures of surplices dating from the fifteenth century show examples of hemstitch; but, as many of its European names suggest, the true origins of lace must be sought elsewhere. The French *dentelle* derives from *dent*, a tooth; the Italian *merletto* from *merlo*, a battlement; while the German *spitz* actually means a point or peak. Throughout the Middle Ages it was customary to snip the edges of pieces of material into points, and the scalloping of the hems of coats, gowns, doublets, and hoods was in fashion for a very long period. It was therefore only logical that linen articles also should be provided with points. As M. Dreger's researches show, the earliest representations of this fashion in art are to

be found in the pictures of Carpaccio, painted in Venice about the year 1500. The Venetian master portrays linen apparel decorated with needleworked points in the form of leaves and stars, and it is possible, indeed probable, that this form of ornament was derived from the East. At the same time, however, the craft of fringe-making that is of securing the projecting warp-threads at the raw edge of the web by plaiting them together, also exercised an influence. This device was known to the Assyrians and Babylonian and was passed on by them to the Greeks. By the systematic

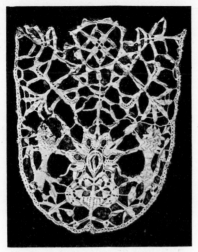

NEEDLE-WORKED POINT
Sixteenth-Century Italian

plaiting and knotting of such threads in oblique and tranverse
lines points are obtained, and in this way probably arose the
"lace" on table-cloths and table-napkins. It was closely akin
to bobbin- or pillow-lace which is in essence no more than the
extreme exploitation of the possibilities of plaiting. We now
see the double source of the craft of lace-making; bobbin-lace
has developed from fringe-making; needle-point from open-
work, which, in the course of development from tiny openings
in the fabric to elaborate designs, with the spaces worked over
in bars, points, and curves, became hardly distinguishable from
true lace.

A glance at the literature of the subject might at first suggest
that lace-making was a German invention, since the earliest
pattern-books appeared in Germany. The first known to us
was published in Zwickau, in 1525, by Gottfried Leigel, a pupil
of Cranach, the next in Cologne, in 1527, by Peter Quentel.
Dreger, however, shows that these publications, as well as
those issued in Venice in 1530-1, deal not with true lace, but
with plaiting, netting, and embroidery. Developments of

3

COLLAR AND POINTS. *Sixteenth-Century Italian*

open-work in linen, which appeared in the Netherlands about the year 1500, have given rise to speculation as to whether the technique of lace-making may not perhaps have originated there, possibly at the same time as in Italy. The greater probability, however, speaks for Italy. In a pattern-book published in Zurich, in 1561-2, by Christopher Froschauer, the designer states that Venetian merchants brought the art of bobbin-lace to Switzerland in 1536, and that it was "at first used only for shirts, but now also for collars, sleeves, coifs, caps, handkerchiefs, table- and bed-linen." Queen Eleanor of France, consort of Francis I, wore open-work and *points*; and in 1455 "fine lace from Florence for trimming collars," is mentioned in an inventory of the possessions of Queen Margaret of Navarre.

The earliest more elaborate designs in lace were executed in bobbin-lace, and at first were frequently carried out in two or more colours. As the craft spread, however, which it did rapidly, the use of a single colour prevailed. Many reasons combined to make bobbin-lace popular. The work is not difficult, while the result is pleasing, and it had this great advantage over the gold lace employed hitherto, that it could be washed. Great ladies, who had nothing but needlework wherewith to pass the long leisure hours, took up pillow-lace

4

BOBBIN-LACE. *Sixteenth-Century Italian*

with enthusiasm. The inventory (1571-2), of Philippine Welser of Ambras mentions a green velvet pillow "on which Her Ladyship makes lace." At the same time among the lower orders it became a means of livelihood so welcome that Philip II actually thought it advisable to prohibit lace-making in the Netherlands in 1590, lest the people should cease altogether to hire themselves out for domestic service. About 1560, Barbara Uttmann, *née* Etterlein, introduced the manufacture of galloon into Annaberg, in Saxony, while bobbin-lace probably first became known there through the work-people who came from Flanders in 1561.

Parallel with the naturalisation of bobbin-lace in Germany went the development in Italy of needle-point, at that time known by the delightful name of *punto in aria*, "stitch in the air." Pattern-books issued in Venice in the second half of the sixteenth century helped to improve the art of needle-point. Between 1562 and 1599 a number of works were published, the majority of which went into several editions. Cesare Vecellio, a brother of Titian, is acquainted with "open-work with points" (lace, in fact), "such as is now in use everywhere in Europe." Giacomo Franco gives beautiful patterns of drawn thread-work. The numerous editions enjoyed by these publications within a short space of time testify to the need which they so fortunately supplied. Womankind

5

VENETIAN LACE APRON
Sixteenth Century

was, it is clear, only too grateful for a species of handiwork
so conspicuously pleasing in its results; and nuns, in particular,
sought useful employment for their spare hours in the manufacture of lace. "Convent lace," was a much sought-after
article down to the nineteenth century.

In the matter of design, geometrical devices predominated,
intermingled with figures of beasts and men and varied by
flowers and plants strictly stylised. The use of lace for collars,
and cuffs ensured the prevalence of pointed forms, and as it
was often used gathered or puckered together the designs
must be simple to be effective. It is only in the Netherlandish

6

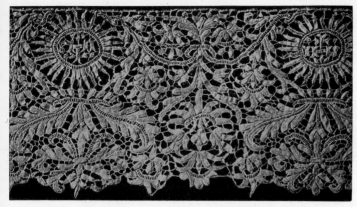

NEEDLE-POINT OF THE LATER ITALIAN RENASCENCE TYPE
First Half of the Seventeenth Century

needle-point laces that the flower-, tendril- and vase-motives
are often so thickly clustered that the effect produced is that
of a very thin fabric, while the essential "laciness" is somewhat
lost.

It was early discovered how to blend the two techniques.
For example, what is called "point lace" is a lace in which
the main features of the design are made upon a pillow, while
the connecting links are supplied by the needle.   The gold and
silver laces, so often mentioned in the sixteenth century, came
from Genoa or Milan and are really fringe-work in gold and
silver threads; what was then called "point d'Espagne" was
more akin to embroidery.   Before the end of the sixteenth
century lace-making was known and practised widely, but it
was not easy for other European countries to compete with
the Netherlands.   That country produced the finest flax and
possessed the best methods of bleaching; its thread could not
be matched, far less surpassed, for fineness and lustre.   England,
too, attempted to make lace, but found it necessary to import
the thread from Holland.

Had the use of lace been confined to the trimming of underlinen its manufacture would hardly have grown to the dimensions
which it very speedily reached.   But the sixteenth century's

7

NEEDLE-POINT LACE. *England, Seventeenth Century*

most conspicuous article of adornment, the ruff, positively cried out for lace, so that on all sides the demand was almost greater than the supply could satisfy. As Mrs. Bury Palliser has shown, there are entries for lace of all sorts in vast quantity in Queen Elizabeth's wardrobe accounts, after 1558; and not only did lace play an important part in the toilet of the Sovereign, but, in Elizabeth's day, that article could be found even in the stores of petty dealers in the English provinces. It is common knowledge that the Virgin Queen loved finery and display as dearly as any woman who ever graced a throne. She wore her ruffs higher, stiffer, and of greater circumference than anyone else in Europe. In England this fashion was called French; in France, on the other hand, they talked of "those English monstrosities." In her portraits Elizabeth is shown sumptuously adorned with lace; ruffs, cuffs, veils, all are trimmed with it. She also liked greatly to receive gifts in this costly material; and the products of her own realm being insufficient to satisfy her, she welcomed the laces of Italy and Flanders. Sir Philip Sidney made her presents of foreign

8

FLEMISH BOBBIN-LACE COLLAR. *Seventeenth Century*

laces, while, soon after her accession, the Countess of Worcester gave her a ruff trimmed with lace and set with rubies and pearls. Probably the delight the exalted lady took in lace was the reason why she issued strict edicts in 1562 and 1573 against its use as an article of attire; she wanted to keep the luxury to herself! Mary Stuart, Elizabeth's rival, seems to have used no lace except on her bedclothes.

Gold lace was preferred to linen lace as a trimming for

BOBBIN-LACE COLLAR, PERHAPS SPANISH. *Seventeenth Century*

9

COLLAR OF VENETIAN NEEDLE-POINT. *Seventeenth Century*

gowns and coats, and must, indeed, have been better suited to the heavy damask and brocade fabrics of those days. We read that after the death of Queen Catherine of Poland a red velvet under-dress "trimmed all over with gold and silver lace" was found among her possessions. At the parliament of Blois in 1577, King Henry III wore four thousand yards of real gold lace on his person. In the seventeenth century Mme d'Aulnoy writes that the Spanish ladies wear a dozen or more petticoats, each more beautiful than the other, made of rich material and trimmed right up to the waist-band with gold and silver lace. Gabrielle d'Estrées, who died (of poisoning it is supposed) in 1599, left lace of such great value that her royal lover, Henry IV, insisted on its being returned to him.

The seventeenth and eighteenth centuries may justly be called the golden age of lace. The sexes rivalled each other

10

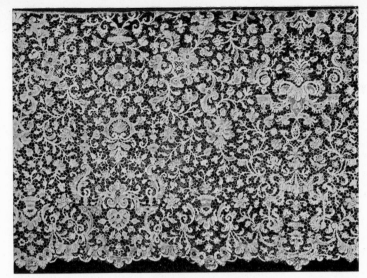

in its extravagant use. They wore it on all their underwear, for a long period on their outer garments; and, often as the mode changed, lace always remained in fashion. Its use was not discontinued by men till the French Revolution.

About the end of the sixteenth century, and the beginning of the seventeenth, the ruff attained enormous proportions and was made preferably of lace. King James I of England used twenty-five yards for a single ruff, his consort, eighteen yards. Gentlemen's shirts were trimmed with lace, and had lace insertions. After the assassination of Henry IV, the shirt, lace-trimmed at throat and wrists, through which the murderer's steel had found him, was publicly displayed on one of the boulevards. Charles I of England at one time bought a thousand yards of lace for the collars and cuffs of his shirts and six hundred yards for his night-shirts; in 1625 he gave £1000 for lace, and in 1633 £1500.

In the first decades of the seventeenth century the ruff gave place to wide lace collars, worn by ladies and gentlemen alike, so that at a ball in Augsburg it was possible for Gustavus Adolphus to take off his collar and place it as a special act of

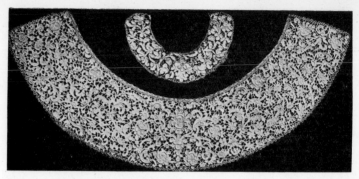

COLLAR OF VENETIAN "PUNTO A RILIEVO" (RELIEF LACE)
Second Half of the Seventeenth Century

homage round the shoulders of Josephine Lauber, the ball-room queen of the evening. In London in 1638 such an article would cost from three to four pounds sterling, and a French courtier said of himself with pride "I am wearing thirty-two acres' worth of the very best vineyards round my neck." But for gentlemen this was not all; they filled the wide tops of their low riding boots with thickly-pleated lace, called in France "canons." The Marquis de Cinq-Mars, whose handsome head Richelieu caused to be laid at his feet one fine day in 1642, left three hundred pairs of such trimmings. With shoes long bands about the knees were worn, trimmed with lace at the ends, and rosettes of lace adorned the shoes themselves. At that time the price of such rosettes in England varied from about thirty shillings to three pounds a pair. Peacham mentions a pair valued at about fifteen pounds, so that a Puritan member of the House of Commons could assert with some show of truth that these shoe-rosettes cost the son more than a whole suit of clothes had cost the father. The body of Louis XIII lay on the bier clad in a resplendent shirt of lace. Ladies wore just such wide lace collars as gentlemen, with, in addition, lace cuffs, lace aprons, lace-trimmed caps and underwear. It is plain, from the pictures which Abraham Bosse has left us of elegant society in his day, that not only did ladies and gentlemen wear a superfluity of lace about their

12

PORTRAIT OF AGATHA GELVINCK

persons, but that table and bed-linen was lavishly adorned with the same. It was used unsparingly, too, for children's clothes and the tiny bibs and caps were never without lace.

The industry—principally a home industry—kept many hands busy. In the Île de France in 1634, the children in more than ten thousand families were occupied in lace-making and it was much the same in Auvergne. A great deal of lace was also made in Sedan, which belonged to France after 1641, and no less in Alençon.

Even so the supply was insufficient to meet the demand, and many countries, particularly England and France, were obliged to import lace in large quantities. Seeing that vast sums of good money were going abroad in exchange for an article of pure luxury, the governments concerned embarked on repressive measures, which were however, in some cases, so severe as to kill the home industry also. Ruin stared the lace-makers of the Auvergne in the face when a Jesuit father, Franciscus Regis, espoused their cause with energy and success. He died

13

CRAVAT-END IN NEEDLE-POINT. PROBABLY BRUSSELS WORK
Early Eighteenth Century

in 1640 and on his canonisation by Rome the grateful lace-makers chose him for their patron.

Louis XIV had in his minister Colbert a man with real genius for political economy, a man who fully realised that flat prohibition is useless and that to wrestle successfully with evil social or economic conditions it is necessary to proceed creatively. Accordingly, he revivified the French lace industry by getting women lace-makers to come from Venice, and so founded in Alençon a trade which was to become deservedly famous through the lace named after the city of its origin. He had many obstacles to surmount. The Venetian Senate, in the first place, was provoked at the loss of its most highly-skilled workers, for since all nuns and the majority of the poorer families in Venice in 1664 lived on lace-making, the transplantation of that industry to France was bound to cause great losses to the Republic. As a first step the emigrants were summoned to return, but vigorous measures were resorted to when they took no notice of the summons. The nearest

14

BOBBIN-LACE TRIMMING FOR AN ALB
Brussels. Early Eighteenth Century

Valenciennes
BOBBIN-LACE LAPPET
Mid-Eighteenth Century

relatives of such as would not return were cast into prison and were to be put to death in case of continued obduracy.

This difficulty, however, was not the only one that Colbert had to meet. The company which he founded in 1665 engaged French workwomen, but these proved obdurate in the extreme when it was suggested to them that they should do their work differently and follow patterns different from those to which they were accustomed. A report informed the minister that, of eight thousand workwomen, seven hundred at most were willing and amenable, but that of these seven hundred no more than two hundred and fifty were fit to be entrusted with the work. As, however, in the meantime the French Court had taken a fancy to "points d'Alençon," Colbert had won the game; France was no longer forced to import lace and soon began to export it.

At first the French lace-makers imitated the Venetian, but they soon evolved a style of their own. Points disappeared and a single dominating motive, usually a continuous wreath, supplanted to a large extent the use of often rather trivial separate detail. The patterns became more delicate and the background more important.

The lace collars of the early seventeenth century dwindled to cravats, in the case

16

Mechlin
BOBBIN-LACE LAPPET
Early Eighteenth Century

of masculine wear, as the century advanced, for when huge periwigs covered the back and shoulders the lace could only show on the breast. Louis XIV liked to give such cravats as presents. The average price paid for these articles of attire by Charles II of England and his brother, James II, was twenty pounds sterling. In the days of Anne of Austria the collar, as worn by women, had become the *berthe*, which surrounded the neck of the gown. In order to display their wealth of lace, the ladies resorted to fancy aprons, made entirely of lace. In 1674, Mme de Sévigné saw one for the first time; it was worn by Mme de Blois. In 1698, the Duchess of Burgundy wore a lace apron worth a thousand pistoles at the fêtes held in Versailles to celebrate her marriage. Ladies' caps were also made of lace and they

C   17

ALENÇON NEEDLE-POINT
Second half of the Eighteenth Century

had their dresses trimmed with the costliest kinds. At a
certain court entertainment which he gave at Marly, Louis XIV
surprised every lady present with the gift of a gown, trimmed
with the most exquisite lace. Underlinen was lavishly
adorned with lace, though, indeed, the underlinen itself was
often sadly to seek. When Pope Clement IX on his election
to the Papacy sent a present of fine lace cuffs to a certain
M. de Sorbière with whom he had been friendly as Cardinal,
the latter cried out in his disappointment, "He sends me lace
when I have no shirts!"

By the last third of the century black lace had become
modish in France. For example, ladies wore gowns of black
lace over gold or silver brocade. The demand for lace was so
great that the annual consumption in France early in the
eighteenth century was estimated at eight million francs' worth.

In 1662, England, on grounds of political economy, strictly
prohibited the import of foreign lace, with the result that
lace-smuggling became a flourishing trade. Brussels lace
were imported by an evasion of the law and then sold as good

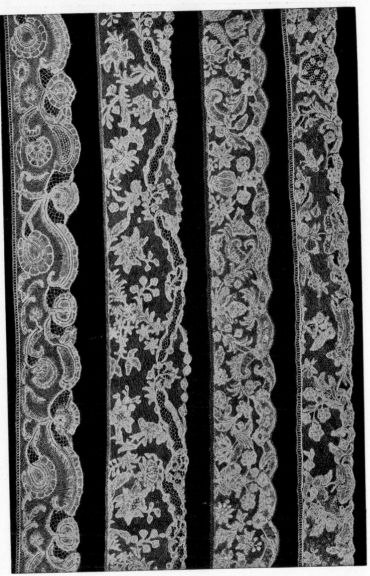

BRUSSELS LACE. *Eighteenth Century*

19

BELGIAN NEEDLE-POINT. *Late Eighteenth Century*

of English origin. Mme d'Aulnoy tells us that the single white petticoat—the "sabenque"—worn by Spanish ladies must be trimmed with English lace. "So great is their vanity," writes the Frenchwoman, "that they would rather have one of these lace petticoats then a dozen ordinary ones, and they will stay in bed while it is being washed, or go without altogether, as, indeed, they do frequently enough." One of these fashionable petticoats might cost as much as six hundred florins or more. In 1678 the Marquis de Nesmond seized a ship bound for England and took from her, besides lace fans, collars, fichus, aprons and petticoats, eight hundred thousand yards of Brussels lace.

As for kings and princes, they did not let laws enacted by their parliaments influence them in the least, and vast quantities of Venetian and Netherlandish laces appear in the wardrobe accounts of Charles II and James II. In 1694, William III spent £1918 on lace, and in the following year £2459, sums

20

BRUSSELS LACE. *Early Nineteenth Century*
From an Alb of Cardinal Fesch

which include expenditure on lace trimmings for such articles
as shaving towels and napkins.   After 1698 the laws against
the import of foreign lace were more strictly enforced, but the
Court was not affected.   Queen Anne, the last of the Stuarts,
paid £247 in 1713 for eighty-three yards of Malines lace, and
this was to serve merely for the trimming of underlinen and
not for *la grande toilette*.   It may be noted that at that time all
Flanders lace, even when not coming from Mechlin, was
commonly called "Malines," and indeed, as Dreger points out,
the names by which laces are known in trade are by no means
necessarily indicative of their place of origin.

In the eighteenth century Brussels lace beat all other kinds
off the field.   It was so greatly preferred that in 1770, at the
wedding of the son of the Doge of Venice, every lady present
wore Brussels lace and no other, and only the altar-cloth was
trimmed with Venetian lace.   Brussels lace possessed many

PART OF AN "EMPIRE" DRESS IN BLACK SILK BOBBIN-LACE

advantages, not merely the finest and most glossy linen thread, but also the best designs. The ground was either bobbin- or needlepoint-lace; in the latter case it was more durable and less easily pulled out of shape, but it was dearer by one-third. The pattern was worked with the needle, and in the eighteenth century naturalistic designs predominated and became markedly asymmetrical.

For both sexes lace continued to be indispensable. The gentleman's cravat, which was worn for some decades in the form of the "steinkirk," that is, with the under end not fastened but drawn through the button-hole, gave place, it is true, to the "jabot," but cuffs remained and both jabot and cuffs were of lace. "A gentleman is known by the lace he wears," was a saying of those days, and Mercier admits that a man of fashion in Paris might wear a soiled shirt or none at all, but that his jabot and cuffs must be lace of the finest quality. Lace was the customary wedding-gift of the bride

W. von Kaulbach   1831
JOSEPHINE SUTNER, BRIDE OF THE PAINTER

to the bridegroom, and was so essential a part of the toilet of anyone of standing that in France even the executioner mounted the scaffold in lace jabot and cuffs. Lackeys, too, were decked out in it. Casanova, when in funds, would pay fifty louis d'or for a lace shirt. In 1738 the Duc de Penthièvre paid 500 francs for a night-shirt and 250 francs for a night-cap. The Archbishop of Cambrai, who died in 1764, left four dozen pairs of lace cuffs. These were worn so wide that they not only covered the hand but hung far over it, so that the economically-minded Frederick the Great could cut his in half with a pair of paper scissors, as he once did in de Catt's presence, and make two pairs out of one. Even in January 1792, Louis XVI's wardrobe still contained fifty-nine pairs of cuffs. Each cuff took about one and a quarter yards of lace at forty-five francs the yard.

The lady's toilet offered even more opportunities for the display of lace than the gentleman's. Lace aprons were worn

and dresses were ornamented with lace flounces, cascades and sleeve trimmings. The so-called "engageantes"—short under-sleeves terminating at the elbow in lace cuffs—remained in fashion for nearly a hundred years. In 1688, Queen Mary of England paid as much as £30 for a pair, while the Comtesse du Barry bought hers at 8000 francs. Lace mantles were used to cover the *décolleté*, and in 1760 Countess Francisca Crasinska gave a hundred ducats for one. Dresses made entirely of lace became the mode. Maria Theresa, as sovereign of the Netherlands, possessed a magnificent robe of lace, and Madame de Pompadour paid a sum equal to about £3000 in modern money for a dress of "point d'Angleterre." Such gowns were much coveted as wedding-dresses. The Infanta Barbara of Portugal, who married the future Ferdinand III of Spain, dedicated the robe of lace she wore for the ceremony to Our Lady in Lisbon Cathedral, but, later, when the French took that capital, Junot carried it off and gave it to his wife. The

24

NEEDLE-POINT. *Nineteenth Century*

25

Countess Barbara Crasinska, who was married in February 1759, wore a wedding-dress of white atlas, entirely covered with Brabant lace, and Countess Waldner, at her marriage to Baron Oberkirch in 1786, wore one of Venetian lace over white satin. In 1804 Napoleon sent two lace gowns to Berlin, one for Queen Louise and one for the wife of the Prime Minister, with instructions to Beurnonville, the French ambassador, to see that the less beautiful of the two went to the Queen.

Underlinen, bedlinen, bath-towels, wraps for hair-dressing —all were trimmed with lace, while the little caps worn by women about the house were made entirely of lace, and the long trailing ribbons, the "barbes" or pinners, which confined the coiffure, were also of lace. These "barbes" were an important item of the toilet, and it was exactly prescribed for the ladies of the French Court when they might let them hang and when they must pin them up.

Lace was a most essential part of a lady's outfit, and when Louis XV's daughter married the Duke of Parma in 1739 she required 625,000 francs to spend on lace alone. Even in 1786, when the fashion of lace was waning somewhat, Indian muslin having become the mode, Swinburne, writing from Paris, says that the trousseau of a fashionable bride always contained

MANTLE OF BRUSSELS LACE. *Paris International Exhibition, 1867*

26

£5000 worth of lace. In 1768, Hammond of Nottingham had invented a machine capable of producing the ground of lace, the so-called "fond de Bruxelles," a fabric later to be known as tulle, while in 1756, blond-lace, that is, lace made of silk, had appeared in the market. These three novelties, muslin, tulle and blond-lace, displaced linen lace for a time in the favour of the ladies. The gentlemen remained true to lace in so far as the higher clergy still insisted on having albs adorned with broad bands of it. Cardinal de Rohan, to whom the "neck-lace case" brought an unhappy notoriety, gave one hundred thousand francs for a single beautiful alb.

During the second half of the eighteenth century the patterns worked in linen-thread lace tended to become somewhat lighter and thinner. The Louis Seize style favoured designs formed of scattered little sprigs of flowers, airy garlands and tendrils. But the use of lace in the toilet had already fallen off considerably before the French Revolution brought it to an abrupt end. In France the lace industry practically disappeared; thirty factories closed down altogether and the workers emigrated, chiefly to Belgium. As civil order was once more restored, lace reappeared, at least for use upon underlinen.

MANTLE OF BRUSSELS LACE. *Paris International Exhibition, 1867*

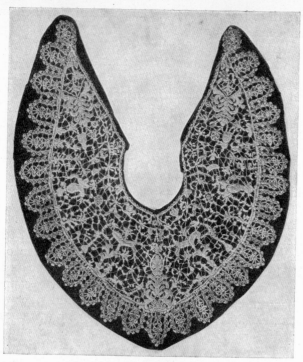

LACE COLLAR. *Seventeenth Century*

Madame Récamier, whose apartments were considered one of the sights of Paris, had the canopy over her bed trimmed with the finest Brussels lace, and the gossipy Duchesse d'Abrantès tells us that all the underlinen in her trousseau (she married in 1800) was trimmed with lace. Napoleon, at his espousals with the Archduchess Marie Louise, placed orders for lace for bed-linen in Alençon. He attempted to revive the almost vanished industry of lace-making and especially patronised Alençon, Chantilly and Brussels. For full Court dress he reintroduced the lace cravat for men. The ladies wore dresses wholly of lace and Marie Louise had a gown in her trousseau worth 5000 francs.

Lace passed through its real revolution in the nineteenth

28

MIXED LACE CRAVAT-END, COLLAR AND NEEDLE-POINT   *Brussels*
Late Nineteenth Century

century. After 1832 cotton thread began to oust linen thread.
Machine-made lace became established after 1837, increasing
the range of use, but lowering the level of importance. Hand-
made lace, as a work of art, is now restricted to a small public,
and machine-made lace holds practically all the field. Certain
great ladies have from time to time endeavoured to revive
the lace industry. Queen Victoria, for instance, had her bridal
gown made of Honiton lace at the cost of £1000, and she also

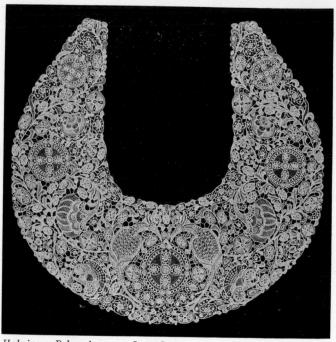

Hedwig von Dobeneck   LACE COLLAR

equipped her daughters, the Princesses Victoria, Alice, and Alexandra with this lace of English manufacture. The Empress Eugénie revived the lace industry in Alençon, whose products found especial favour with the beautiful Spaniard. Her trousseau contained a flounce of Alençon lace upon which thirty-six women had been employed for eighteen months, and which cost 22,000 francs. In 1867 the Empress purchased a lace dress for 70,000 francs. At the International Exhibition of 1867 a dress of "point d'Alençon" was displayed which had cost forty women seven years' work and which was priced at 85,000 francs. In 1856 the Empress ordered an entire layette of Alençon lace for the child whose birth she was expecting. Orders for trousseaux came from Russia to the value of 150,000 francs.

Nineteenth-century fashions were very favourable to the

use of lace. The crinoline was admirably adapted for a brilliant display of laces of every pattern and width; flounces and over-dresses wholly of lace were in general favour. In addition to white laces, black Chantilly lace was much worn from the thirties onwards. The lace mantilla was long in fashion, in competition with the shawl. Indeed, the toilet afforded numerous opportunities for lace. Then, for a great many years, its use was practically restricted to the petticoat, and now that this has disappeared there remains no place for it except as trimming for the most intimate articles of underwear. Fashion, however, is a capricious dame and will no doubt some day change her mind!

FLOUNCE OF FLEMISH NEEDLE-POINT. *Modern*

After Lepsius

THE PHARAOH HAREMHÊB CARRIED BY SOLDIERS, PRECEDED
AND FOLLOWED BY FAN-BEARERS

CHAPTER II

FANS

THE fan has at least three distinct aspects, as an accessory of religious ceremonial, an everyday necessity, and an implement of coquetry, and has been in use from very early times among uncivilised as among civilised peoples. It is, indeed, far more than a mere plaything, for even in its simplest and most primitive form it serves a great variety of purposes, being used to shield the eyes from the sun's glare, to drive away noxious insects, to fan fire into flame, to cool the air, etc. The needs which called it into being must very early have established a place for it in the court ceremonial of Eastern potentates. The fan was a necessity to them, yet their dignity forbade them to wield it themselves and the task was delegated to others. Certain inferior slaves were told off for this duty, and that affected the shape of the fan which was accordingly fashioned like a whisk of huge dimensions set at the end of a long handle, to be carried and kept in motion before the

32

A GREEK LADY WITH A FAN

Detail from a hydria found at Kertch
The Hermitage, St. Petersburg

countenances of the great. In the palace at Persepolis Persian bas-reliefs represent the king on his throne with slaves standing behind him bearing whisks. This custom, indeed, obtains throughout the East and was as general in Assyria as in India and Egypt. Instances of it have been discovered in the tombs of Egyptian kings dating back to about seventeen hundred years before Christ.

The West imported the custom from the East and, in one place at least, retains it to this very day; for when the Pope takes part in any great procession, fans of peacock's feathers are carried beside his chair. Peacock's feathers they must be, as this bird, regarded by the ancients as a symbol of vanity, became for the early Church a type of modesty; for, when it spreads its tail, it looks not at the gorgeous display of its own plumage, but down at its feet, which are large and coarse and the very opposite of beautiful!

For private use, the earliest fans were no doubt fronds plucked from whatever large-leaved tree grew nearest. Homer, Anacreon and other Greek poets place a fan in the hand of Venus, and we may feel sure that the tender Calypso, the seductive Circe and the virtuous Penelope were all accustomed to enhance their charms by making play with a palm leaf. Numberless Tanagra figures witness to the skill with which the Greek lady manipulated this weapon, the artists rendering most vividly the grace of their beautiful contemporaries

D

QUEEN
THEODOLINDA'S
WHEEL-FAN,
ONE-QUARTER
UNFURLED
Seventh Century?

*From
the Cathedral
Treasury at
Monza*

as they toyed with the leaf-shaped fans.

The Roman ladies adopted the fan (as, indeed, other expressions of Greek culture) from their neighbours. But Roman luxury did not rest content with leaves as nature offered them. The fan retained, it is true, the form of a large curved leaf, but it was made of thin wood, delicately carven, gaily painted and gilded. Feather fans also are portrayed in monumental carvings, peacock's feathers being preferred to all other kinds and most fans having very long handles. Fashionable ladies kept special slaves to attend them with fans and keep the air in cooling motion about them. No actual fans survive from antiquity. Although Forrer found flag-shaped fans, rectangular and plaited in straws of divers colours to form patterns, in the Egyptian tombs at Akhmim, these belong to Byzantine times. The blades of these fans are secured to the handles by cross lacings. This particular form of fan is of great antiquity and an occasional example of it may be found on Chaldean cameos, Greek vases and early Christian golden goblets.

In the early Middle Ages, curiously enough, the fan seems to have disappeared as an accessory of the lady's toilet, its use surviving only in the Church. The Roman rite adopted it from the Eastern Church, where the deacon had the task of guarding the Host from flies and other insects by the use of a fan shaped like a seraph with six wings. The Western Church retained this custom, although under the

34

FLABELLUM FROM
TOURNUS ABBEY,
FRANCE
Ninth Century ?

*The Bargello,
Florence*

FLABELLUM IN THE
SPITZER COLLECTION

Fifteenth Century

35

FASHION-PLATE
Bertuch's " Journal des Luxus und der Moden," June, 1800

climatic conditions of the regions where it held sway the need for protection against winged pests was less obviously urgent than in the hot countries of the East. From the ninth century church inventories frequently make mention of the "flabellum ad muscas a sacrificiis abigendas." In 831 the church of St. Riquier possessed a silver fan for this purpose; in 1244 there was one of silk in Salisbury Cathedral and in 1298 one of peacock's feathers in St. Paul's, London. An inventory of the treasures of the Holy See taken in 1295 under Pope Boniface VIII, mentions ten different fans, large and small, made of gilded parchment, silk, aloe-wood and peacock's feathers, all of them round, with wooden handles.

By fortunate chance some of these ancient ritual fans have been preserved. One from the Abbey of Tournus passed from the Carrand collection into the possession of the Bargello in Florence. The blade, which is made of painted wood, is round and can be folded; when folded it slips into an ivory case attached to a long ivory handle. The age of this remarkable relic is a matter of controversy, although the maker has inscribed his name upon his work in the words " Johel me sancte fecit in honore Mariae." Some would like to attribute it to the ninth century, but others, including Viollet-le-Duc, incline to the twelfth. Molinier points out that the aforesaid Johel has probably made use of the sides of an ancient casket and

36

that we cannot attribute to his hand the figures thereon, Apollo and Admetus, Apollo and Marsyas, and Silenus in which the treatment of the nude points to a much earlier period. The figures of the Blessed Virgin, St. Agnes, St. Philibert and St. Peter, to be seen on the upper part, are certainly by another hand. A similar fan exists in the treasury of Monza Cathedral and is said to have been presented to the church about 590 by Theodolinda, wife of Autharis, the Lombard king.

FRAU V. VON A., *née* R. VON B.
Potsdam, 1871

The blade of this fan is made of strong, thin parchment, coloured a deep violet; upon this purple background designs and letters are painted in gold and silver. Unfurled, it is wheel-shaped, but when closed it can be drawn into a case made of soft wood plated with silver and chased with romanesque floral designs. Franz Bock is inclined to date the fan from the time of the Ottos, the tenth or eleventh century, rather than from the sixth. If a donor must be found, Bock prefers the Empress Theophano, who might well have brought the fan with her from Byzantium. In the Spitzer collection there is a similar fan, dated by the owner no earlier than the fifteenth century. Its blade measures thirty centimetres in diameter and is made of parchment with a cross-shaped decoration in blue and gold painted upon it. The stem is boxwood, the actual handle showing a kind of plaited mesh, while the upper portion forms an octagonal case with gothic niches containing the figures of Saints James, Peter, Dominic, Magdalene, Catherine, Cecilia, and others. This specimen comes from Spain. The round shape is interesting as it is one which constantly recurs.

37

A Young Girl of the Fugger
Family, Augsburg *c.* 1550

A Lady of Lyons
c. 1550

It would not be easy to say at exactly what period women
recovered the use of the fan. They may have owed its
reacquisition to the Crusades. If the Crusaders did not find
in the Holy Land those treasures they went to seek, they did
at least, through their contact with Eastern peoples, experience
the strong stimulus of a foreign culture, and that most notably
in all matters of care of the person, clothing, etc. Thus they
may have learned the use of the fan. As might be expected,
it first reappears among the very highest ranks of society, in
the hands of women of noble blood. Mention is made of it
in contemporary romances of chivalry as early as the thirteenth
and fourteenth centuries. In 1316 the Comtesse d' Artois had
a fan with a handle of solid silver, and in 1328 Queen Clémence
of France possessed one richly embroidered in silk. In 1372
Queen Jeanne d'Évreux left at her death a fan of gold brocade,
embroidered with the lilies of France and the arms of France
and Navarre, set in a handle of ivory and jet. It was valued
at five gold francs, an immense sum for those days.

38

PORTRAIT OF HIS DAUGHTER, LAVINIA SARCINELLI, BY TITIAN

The shape of these fans is uncertain. As, however, they are called "esmouchoirs"—that is to say fly-whisks—in the old French inventories, they may probably be rightly thought of as whisks with long handles, such as were employed in church at Mass. For the ladies who owned them did not use them personally; either they were wielded for their benefit by servants, or else they were simply adjuncts of their private chapels. In an inventory of the goods of Isabeau of France, Queen of England, dated 1359, two articles "pro muscis fugandis" are entered among the accessories of her chapel, not among those of her toilet or her jewelry.

An inventory of the goods of Charles V of France, dated 1380, is evidential as to the form and use of the fan. It records "flags to drive away flies from the King when he is at table."

39

FLAG-FAN OF
ITALIAN PLAITED
STRAW WITH AN
IVORY HANDLE

*National Museum,
Munich, c. 1560*

These little flags are described as being made
of cut leather with silver-gilt handles. This
is the first instance of the reappearance of
the flag-shaped fan, the least practical shape,
perhaps, which that article has ever assumed,
but popular, no doubt on account of its
novelty, for in 1416 and 1417 the Queen of
France purchased several specimens of the
kind. King Charles V had also another fan,
"round, of ivory, capable of being folded,
bearing the arms of France, with a handle
of ebony." It thus appears to have been
shaped like the liturgical fans and to have
been constructed of separate spokes. Viollet-
le-Duc found such spokes among the burnt-
out ruins of Pierrefonds Castle, dating from
a period earlier than 1422.

The whisk-like fan, however, still persisted. In 1480 the Queen of Sicily received
one made of peacock's feathers, and they are
to be found occasionally even in the sixteenth
century. Andreas von Blumental, of the
commandery of Wildenbruch in Pomerania,
who died in 1560, left two "fly-whisks," one
of peacock's feathers, one of wood. When the widowed Queen
Elizabeth of France, who had been an Austrian Archduchess,
died in 1593, there was among her possessions an "Indian fly-
whisk made of feathers, very beautiful and cunningly wrought."
"Indian," of course means West Indian, for in the new Indies the
art of working in feathers had attained the height of perfection.
The ill-fated Montezuma sent Cortes a present of two fans of
marvellous feather-work with golden handles. It was not
till the sixteenth century that the "whisk" gave place to the
genuine "fan," when that implement finally took its place in
the lady's own hand and was no longer left to servants to scare
flies; at the same time art and craftsmanship took charge of
its shaping and decoration.

40

PLATE II

ROCOCO FAN, PAINTED IN BODY-COLOURS

French 18th Century.   In the possession of Fraulein E. von Sichart.   Munich

Agostino Caracci *Bologna, c.* 1580
DESIGN FOR AN OSTRICH-FEATHER FAN

Hitherto there had been three shapes—the "whisk," the "flag" and the "wheel." The whisk was a rigid blade with a handle of greater or lesser length fastened thereto at the centre of its lower edge; the flag had its handle fastened at one side, the wheel was the only one of the three which could be folded. Now there were as many new shapes as materials. The blade was made circular, semi-circular, square or octagonal. To wood and feathers were added parchment, paper, leather, and silk, supplemented, later on, by chicken- and swan-skin, tulle and lace. In addition to ivory, mother-of-pearl and tortoiseshell were used, and curling ostrich feathers began to oust bright-coloured peacock's feathers. But, most important of all, the folding fan appeared in the sixteenth century. The wheel was known already, but now

41

A FAMILY CELEBRATION (detail)

people were content with a semi- or quarter-circle without a
distinct handle.   At first the new fan was like one of those toys
that children, to this day, make for themselves out of paper by
creasing it first to the right and then to the left, so that when
it is held fast at the bottom it spreads of itself above into a
fan-shaped form.   In its origins it could be compared with a
"harlequin's sword," which, indeed, may actually have stood
godfather to it, so great is their similarity.   Below, it ended
in a round knob, convenient to the grasp.

The folding fan as we know it to-day, consisting of a series

Moreelse   *The Hague,* 1627
PORTRAIT OF A LADY

of long narrow blades connected by a band, or of thin spokes over which a wide covering sheet has been plastered, is of Oriental, not of European, origin. As far as it may be traced, it appears to have come to Europe by way of Spain. In an inventory dated 1569 of the Archduke Ferdinand of Tyrol, the husband of Philippine Welser, are mentioned "two Spanish whisks which can be opened and shut," and the dowager Queen Elizabeth of France left in 1593 twelve "Spanish fly-whisks from Ebano." The folding fan probably derives from Japan and reached Europe by way of China in the course of trade. In both Japan and China, it is held to be of the greatest antiquity. There it is—or was till a few decades ago—

43

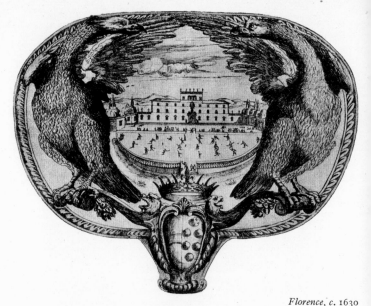

A PAPER FAN, SHOWING A GAME OF BALL OUTSIDE VILLA POGGIO A CAIANO
From a design by Étienne de la Belle

considered indispensable for persons of both sexes and was an article of mass production. In Canton a thousand fans ready for use could be bought for nine francs. In Japan at one time the army carried iron fans, which were used in drill like swords. Soldiers even saluted with them. In Spain (which it may possibly have reached by way of Portugal) the fan made itself almost equally indispensable, and even now in that peninsula one never meets a person of the female sex without one. Even children in arms play with tiny folding fans.

Nevertheless the whisk- and flag-like forms maintained their existence side by side with the new-fashioned folding fan, attractive and practical as this was, perhaps because they offered more scope for luxurious developments. The Archduchess Margaret, daughter of the Emperor Maximilian I, left at her death in 1530 a number of brilliant feather fans,

44

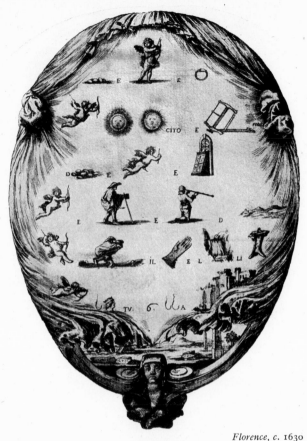

Florence, c. 1630

PAPER FAN WITH REBUS
Engraved by Étienne de la Belle

among them two particularly gorgeous specimens, one of
peacock's feathers with a centre - piece of gold embroidery
upon carmoisin silk, the other of black feathers stitched with
gold.   Queen Margaret of Navarre, the first wife of Henry IV,
who set the fashion in everything at the French court, appears
to have preferred the whisk-like fan.   In 1583 she possessed
one of white feathers, on one side a little mirror surrounded

45

"THE TRIUMPH OF DAVID," PAPER FAN   *Paris, c.* 1640
Engraved by Nicolas Cochin

by eight rubies "en cabochon" (that is, polished but uncut), on the other, four cameos and a pearl. A fan of this sort might easily be worth a small fortune. Margaret gave a mother-of-pearl fan worth 1200 talers to her sister-in-law, Louise de Lorraine, the wife of Henry III. Of the same material was the whisk-fan Brantôme saw in the hands of Queen Eleanor, wife of Francis I; this also contained a mirror and was set with precious stones of immense value.

The fans brought by Catherine de' Medici from Italy were made of round spokes, with a surround of feathers. During her long life the transition from the whisk-fan to the folding fan was completed, for at her death in 1589 she left five fans of leather, "à la façon du Levant" which can have been no other than folding fans. Catherine's son, King Henry III, hastened this change of fashion, for that effeminate prince had an extraordinary predilection for the fan and influenced even his male courtiers in this respect. A lampoon entitled *The Island of Hermaphrodites* and aimed against the court of

46

this monarch and his male favourites, says: "Into his right hand was put an instrument which could be opened out and refolded by the mere pressure of a finger, and which is called a fan. It was made of parchment, very finely fretted and set round about with points of the same material. It was large enough to be used as a parasol, to guard against sunburn and to fan cooling airs against the delicate skin." Henry III's fans were made of silk, adorned with gold or silver lace.

Queen Elizabeth of England, who loved to deck her person and almost literally covered herself with jewels, extended her favour to the whisk-fan with its possibilities of resplendent decoration. This exalted lady liked to receive fans as presents, and a portrait of her in the Duke of Devonshire's collection shows her with a costly fan in her left hand. When she declared that a fan was the only gift a queen could suitably accept from a subject, people strove zealously to fulfil her wishes. Given handles of gold and gems, it was easy enough to spend forty pounds sterling and more on such articles. These valuables were splendid booty for thieves. "When Mistress Bridget lost the handle of her fan, I took't upon mine honour thou hadst it not," says Falstaff to Pistol in *The Merry Wives of Windsor*. The vain and splendour-loving Elizabeth left at her death thirty fans of the costliest quality.

The whisk-fan was usually made with a rigid centre-piece,

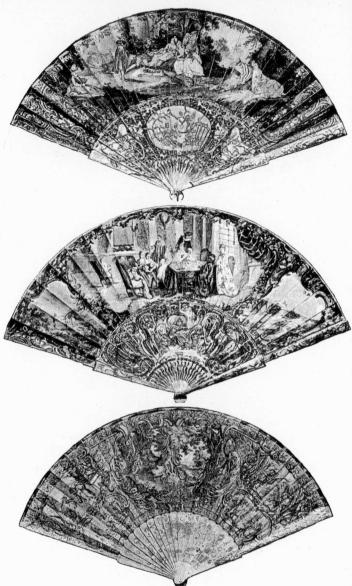

EIGHTEENTH-CENTURY FRENCH ROCOCO FANS. *In the Somzée Collection*

for which purpose mirrors, surrounded with peacock's feathers
were most popular. When fashion began to forsake these
gay-coloured but flat feathers in favour of ostrich feathers, a
new form of fan, like a bouquet, came into being. The long
curled feathers were bound together in a bunch in a long
handle of gold, silver or ivory, sometimes set with diamonds.
In 1508 the Margrave of Burgau left in his will a "golden handle
for a fan," valued at forty-two crowns. This kind of fan
derived from Italy, probably from Venice, for the earliest
pictures showing it are all from the hands of Venetian artists
and portray Venetian ladies. Paris Bordone places one such
in the hand of his proud beauty Violante, while Titian's
daughter, Lavinia Sarcinelli, appears, in all her portraits
as a married woman, with immense fans of ostrich feathers,
and the fashion plates of Boissard, Franco and others
delight in showing Venetian women with feather whisks of
this sort.

It may be taken for granted that this costly fashion was
eagerly taken up on the hither side of the Alps. Queen Anne
of England, consort of James I, possessed a whisk-fan made
of three ostrich feathers of great length.

The flag-shaped fan, on the other hand, totally disappeared
during the course of the sixteenth century. As it derived
from Italy, it persisted longest there. The "ventarola" was
a luxury article which apparently never became popular out-

50

side Italy, and even in Venice, where it originated, it came to be prized only as part of the bridal toilet. When Titian painted Lavinia as a bride he did not forget the little flag-fan. Venetian brides are also shown with the "ventarola" in Cesare Vecellio's book of costume. The blade was made of some fabric, stiffened and fastened immovably to the handle; pictures show embroidered and painted specimens. There is in the Bavarian National Museum a flag-fan of that period the blade of which is formed of an extremely fine plait in straw of two colours, while the dainty handle is of ivory inlaid with strips of ebony. A Venetian flag-fan in the Grand Ducal gallery in Carlsruhe is decorated with fretted parchment over a lattice of ivory.

While the flag-fan did not outlast the sixteenth century the whisk-fan and ostrich-feather bouquet survived it only for a very brief time. Rubens and Van Dyck, it is true, painted such fans in a number of portraits, and when they did so, as in the "Helena Fourment" and the

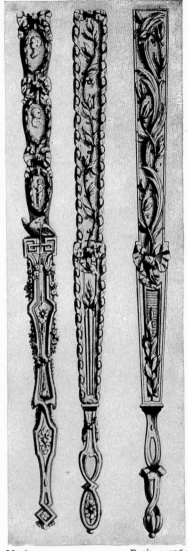

Maria   *Paris, c.* 1760
DESIGNS FOR FAN-HANDLES

"Marie Louise de Tassis," gave

51

us most remarkably fine specimens, but, taken on the whole the folding fan remained victor all along the line. After the first thirty years or so of the seventeenth century it held the field alone. It made its first appearance in the sixteenth century in the hands of those Spanish infantas and great ladies represented upon the canvases of Claudio Coëllo, Pantoja de la Cruz and other Spanish artists, but it must have taken time to acclimatise itself on this side of the Pyrenees, and arrived at first, we may surmise, chiefly in the guise of presents

Two Lacquered Rococo Fans
In the Somzée Collection

to courts allied to the Spanish Habsburgs. Thus the Archduchess Claudia of Tyrol, at Innsbruck in 1628, showed to
Philip Hainhofer a "ventulin" set with diamonds among her
treasures, and the famous Treasury, in Prague, the contents of
which date back to the days of the Emperor Rudolph II, boasted
in 1635 a "ventolo" in ivory, though when later this object
was intended to be sent to Vienna, it turned out that Count
Königsmarck had thought it valuable enough to take with him

Two Lacquered Rococo Fans
In the Somzée Collection

53

to Sweden! Spanish leather fans were also appreciated for
their strong perfume, and as stress was not laid on cleanliness
in those days, no doubt pleasing scents were urgently necessary
to overcome the less agreeable odours everywhere to be en-
countered. The Princesse de Montpensier, writing of Anne of
Austria, the mother of Louis XIV and an infanta of Spain,
says "Although the Queen-Mother always carried a fan of
Spanish leather in her hand, one could smell her wound."

From the mid-seventeenth century onwards, the fan appears
very frequently in popular picture-sheets and illustrations of

TWO LACQUERED ROCOCO FANS
In the Somzée Collection

THE APOTHEOSIS OF KING FREDERICK WILLIAM II. PAPER FAN. 1787
From a design by D. Chodowiecki

modes and manners. About 1640 Abraham Bosse portrayed
the wares on stalls set up by merchants in fashionable goods
in the Palais de Justice in Paris, and there we see numerous
fans, without exception of the folding type. In Wenzel
Hollar's more or less contemporaneous etchings of the modes
and costumes of English ladies, the folding fan regularly appears.
It is even more general in the fashion-plates of Bonnard of
Paris, where it is to be seen closed, half or fully opened, and some
models look entirely modern in construction and decoration.
In less settled communities, where men were perhaps rather a
menace than a protection to women, the fan was capable of becoming a weapon of defence. In the Pola du Rosey collection
there was an ivory fan adorned with the arms and monogram
of Prince Stanislas Radziwill; it would not open, being in fact
merely the scabbard of a dagger whose haft appeared to be
the handle of a fan.

But it was in the eighteenth century that the true era of the
fan began, and from that time it ceased to take any other
shape than that of the folding fan except in the very rarest
instances. If the rococo period marked the reign of Woman,
as has well been said, then the fan was her sceptre and from
it she was inseparable. " Women are armed with fans," wrote
Addison, as men with swords," and it should be remembered
that in those days a gentleman without a sword was an

55

QUEEN MARIE ANTOINETTE'S FAN
Thiac Collection

almost inconceivable phenomenon. All the sex wielded the
fan, from the highest ladies in the land to the women of
the lower orders, but, as Madame de Staël tells us, "the
woman of breeding differs from others in her use of the
fan. Even the most charming and elegant woman, if she
cannot manage her fan, appears ridiculous." Madame de
Staël herself could not do so, but then she was neither elegant
nor charming, merely clever. She never used a fan, but
carried a spray of leaves in her hand to play with and pull
to pieces.

The universal use of the fan established a secure place for
it in social manners and customs. Among the better classes
of society in France it became *de rigueur* for the bride on her
wedding day to present every lady invited with a work-bag
and a fan. It was a fashion from which even princesses were
not exempt. Each had her "corbeille" in which were contained
those objects which it was prescribed she should conscientiously
dispense, strictly according to rank and standing. The thirty-
five fans received by Maria Leczinska on the occasion of her
betrothal to Louis XV on 5 September, 1725, had cost 3,627
francs. Twenty years later her daughter-in-law, the Infanta
of Spain, on a similar occasion received thirty-six fans worth
3,800 francs, while in 1747 the Crown Princess of Saxony was

56

THE APOTHEOSIS OF FREDERICK THE GREAT. PAPER FAN. 1787
From a design by D. Chodowiecki

presented with thirty-seven fans in ivory, mother-of-pearl and wood, ranging in value from twenty-seven to five hundred francs.

The Infanta Isabella of Parma, who in 1760 married the future Emperor Joseph II, was given twenty-four ivory fans to distribute to the ladies. The specimens destined for the exalted brides themselves were, of course, even more costly than the others. The Princess of Saxony received one in gold with two large diamonds valued at 1960 francs, besides which she had already in her trousseau an amethyst fan set with diamonds, and another in mother-of-pearl set with brilliants, rubies and emeralds. The fan in Marie Antoinette's "corbeille," especially destined for herself, was set with diamonds and emeralds. Louis XV was an extravagant parent and presented his daughter, the Duchess of Parma, at the christening of her son, with a carved ivory fan, gilded and set with brilliants, a piece of work priced by the court jeweller at 17,500 francs. By contrast with this, the price of the "extra fine" fan delivered by Gotzkowsky of Berlin to the King of Prussia in 1752 for use as a gift, at a cost of 170 talers (about £25 10s.), sounds quite absurdly modest. Although court etiquette in those days tended to extravagance in the giving of fans, it demanded that the ladies should exercise great restraint in their use. In Versailles fans might not be opened

57

in the presence of the Queen, save, perhaps, for use as a tray whereon to hand Her Majesty some object. It was a great calamity for the Baroness Oberkirch when her fan accidently fell open as she was trying to show Marie Antoinette, who was short-sighted, a bracelet which she was wearing!

Not only ladies of fashion, but lower- and middle-class women also, clung tenaciously to their fans. It is asserted that Charlotte Corday never once let go of her fan during her attempt on Marat. Finally the doctors felt compelled to warn the public against the dangers to health resulting from the misuse of the fan! It is highly entertaining to read what a certain physician has to say on the subject in the *Neue Hamburger Magazin*, 1774. He writes (being prudent enough, however, to remain anonymous) as follows: "Fans—those lovely painted ornaments of lovely hands—are often neither more nor less than sharp knives in the fingers of heedless children. 'Onlooker' (who has brought the drilling of the female in the use of this weapon to a high degree of perfection), and all those fair ones who direct their conduct by my writings, will pardon me, I hope, if, speaking as a doctor, I command them—and rightly—to leave these deleterious instruments at home, or at least to make more sparing use of them for the

ASSIGNATS OF THE FRENCH REPUBLIC.   PRINTED PAPER FAN

uture. It is an established fact that nothing is more dangerous
when the body is heated than to cool some part of it hastily;
yet by means of the fan this sin against the canons of health
is committed unwittingly every day throughout the summer.
How often has not such a proceeding brought high fever,
inflammations, frenzy, and even death in its train? It may
also give rise to certain minor evils, which are, none the less,
troublesome enough. Those headaches, coughs, rheums, con-
gestions and inflammations which females so often bring home
with them from a walk or a visit even on the finest summer
days, more often, perhaps, owe their origin to the use of the
fan than to all those other causes to which they are commonly
ascribed!" But the good doctor's appeal passed as unheeded
as the many anathemas launched at the same period against
tight-lacing.

The widespread use of the fan in all classes of society during
the eighteenth century called an industry into being which
lavishly employed the most various technical processes in the
manufacture of this article of luxury. The most expensive
products went, of course, to ladies of fashion and in 1720 fans
were regularly on sale in the shops of Paris at three to four
hundred francs apiece. These might be of mother-of-pearl,
tortoiseshell, ivory or horn, embroidered "à jour," fret-

59

NAPOLEON BONAPARTE. PRINTED PAPER FAN

worked, carved, engraved, mezzotinted, decorated with metal foil. They were gilded in various tones, the sticks decorated with gold inlay, silver, steel tinsel, etc. The covering of the framework would be preferably of thin parchment, silk, or the so-called "swan's-skin" (which, however, certainly never covered that bird, but was merely a trade term for the finest quality of kid), cut in the form of the segment of a circle and painted in most cases in gouache or body-colour. There are fans in plenty painted by some of the great masters, though of course not all fans decorated with mythological or pastoral scenes after designs by Watteau, Boucher, Lancret, etc., were actually painted by them, even when antique dealers and collectors would have us believe so.

Fan-painting afforded a livelihood, even if not a very prosperous one, for many a second-rate dabbler in brush and water-colour. When Favart, husband of the famous soubrette, was forced to flee because Marshal Saxe was pursuing his wife,

FAN OF QUEEN ELIZABETH OF PRUSSIA, SET WITH SAPPHIRES,
PEARLS AND DIAMONDS
Hohenzollern Heirloom

60

KING FREDERICK WILLIAM III. AND QUEEN LOUISE OF PRUSSIA
PRINTED PAPER FAN

ind threatening him with death, he lived for a year in hiding
n Strasbourg and earned his living by painting fans. Wit
ind ingenuity, banter, gallantry and homage found expression
through the fan. The fair owner could hide her own face
behind it, while at the same time she could see well enough
through tiny windows, sometimes made of magnifying glass.
There were puzzle fans, which showed different pictures according as they were looked at from the left or the right, fans with

FAN CUT IN IVORY
By M. Schwartz of Copenhagen after designs by Thorwaldsen)
A wedding present of the ladies of Copenhagen to the Princess of Wales, 1864

watches in the handle, fans which could be bent in half, far
which would not open until one particular stick was touched
dancing-master's fiddles from which fans could be unfolded
and many other similar amusing devices.

To satisfy the enormous demand Chinese fans were imported
wholesale. They were very durable, being covered in paper
made of bark-fibre, which is stronger than parchment or
fabric. They were, moreover, very cheap. In the middle
of the eighteenth century Lazare Duvaux, the well-known
Paris merchant, sold fifteen Chinese fans for eighteen francs.
In 1752 he delivered to the Marquise de Pompadour a dozen
Nankin fans for seventy-two francs, perhaps the cheapest
purchase that beautiful and extravagant woman ever made
in her life. The competition of the imported Chinese fan with
the home-made article became so serious for the latter that
English fan-makers asked Parliament to prohibit Chinese and
Indian fans from entering the country.

As the painted fan, even when not by the hand of any great
artist, was necessarily an expensive article, the industry met
the demand for picture fans with specimens in copper-plate
on white or tinted paper, at moderate prices. The events of
the day were noted by the makers and everything that captured
the public interest—a man, an event, a discovery, or whatever
else made a stir amongst the ladies—was immediately portrayed
on the paper fan. During the Terror, invention and ingenuity
were exercised to express certain opinions without flaunting
them too publicly, and fans were made which disclosed the
Bourbon lilies only when opened in a particular way. Others
bore the device of a weeping willow, or a basket of white flowers
concealing amidst the leaves profiles of the martyred king and
queen and the poor little dauphin. Or again, the paper notes
issued by the Most Glorious Republic were portrayed in pell-
mell confusion, but closer scrutiny revealed a portrait of
Louis XVI, or some other royalist allusion.

In 1795 there appeared in Paris the so-called "telegraph
fan," by means of which the owner could spell out words
using an alphabet printed on the inner side of the fan and a

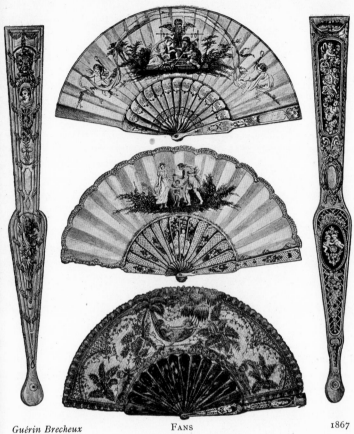

Guérin Brecheux   FANS   1867
Paris International Exhibition

metal pointer projecting a little beyond the sticks. The pleasure of holding a wordless conversation with a person close at hand may seem somewhat childish and boring to us, yet we read in the *Journal des Luxus und der Moden* the report that the Italian, Badini, had so improved upon the telegraph fan, and increased the speed of its use, that Robert Clarke, the foremost London dealer in fans, had taken out a patent on the invention and based a special fan language upon it!

63

EVENING TOILETTE WITH A FEATHER FAN
La Mode Artistique, 1885

In the Empire perio the fan lost none of i popularity, though altered its form som what, becoming ver small and being mor often adorned with gol and silver tinsel tha with paintings. In May 1800, Goethe brough his Christiana a fan fro Carlsbad for which h paid two talers, tw groats. Napoleon gav the Empress Marie Louis as a wedding presen two fans, one set wit diamonds, the other wit diamonds and emeralds the pair costing 9,00 francs. In precious speci mens such as these th two covering sticks alon were set with preciou stones. In 1823 Jorda Bros., the Berlin Court jewellers, made a bridal fan for th Crown Princess Elizabeth, for which they used three hundre brilliants and two hundred and fifty-two small rose-cut stones Queen Elizabeth of Prussia left in her will a sapphire orna ment with a fan to match whose covering blade was set with sapphires and pearls, to remain as heirlooms of the House o Hohenzollern for ever. Fans set with precious stones long remained part of the "grande toilette" of ladies of rank. In 1881 Countess Wallis, *née* Countess Somogyi, gave the Empress Elizabeth a fan set with brilliants, emeralds, rubies and sapphires.

To follow the fashions in fans was difficult, though they

64

PLATE III

PICTURE FAN

FAN

Eduard Grützner

Edmond Morin   FAN WITH AQUARELLE

varied less in ornamentation than in general proportion
and it was ultimately a question of individual taste wheth
a lady preferred feathers, lace, or painting. Under the Secor
Empire, the fan remained of medium size, but was expecte
to make itself conspicuous. In 1857, Bismarck commissione
his sister to buy a fan for his wife Johanna; it was to l
gilt and to rustle a lot! She was to spend ten talers on i
Artists did not cease to expend their talents on adorning th
graceful toy. Gavarni painted a fan for the Empress Eugén
and considered it the best piece of work he had ever don
A novelty was the autograph fan, upon which the fair possesse
collected the autographs of celebrities. This attained i
greatest popularity in the 'seventies. Once only did Fashic
attempt to interest the masculine world in the use of the fa
but the enterprise, begun in Paris in 1828, fell to the groune
Man is too clumsy a creature to handle this charming artic
of coquetry, as many a fan broken by gentlemen at balls an
dances could sadly testify.

Once in the nineteenth century the fan played an histor
role, when in 1827 the Dey of Algiers allowed his temper t
get the better of him at an audience of the French Consu
Duval, and boxed his ears with a fan. France could not swallo

66

his insult and replied by the conquest and annexation of
lgiers. Now the fan belongs to history; it has vanished from
he fashions of our day. Woman has become masculine and
as allowed grace and charm to go by the board. What does
he want with a plaything? She prefers a cigarette. This
hange of outlook explains the numerous exhibitions of fans,
f which nothing was heard while that little instrument was
till in common use. The first of these on a grand scale was
ot up in 1870 by the South Kensington Museum, London,
nder the patronage of the Queen and the nobility. In 1884
Milan followed suit, and in 1891, Carlsruhe. Those exhibitions
mirrored the elegance of a period already long since vanished.

FIDDLE AND WHEEL-FAN
Eighteenth Century

LEATHER GLOVES. *Fourteenth Century*
Probably owned by the Emperor Charles IV

CHAPTER III

GLOVES

THE need for some protection for the hand must have led t
the invention of the glove in very early times. The skins c
beasts would appear to have been the material first used fo
it, and we read that Rebecca made her son Jacob gloves o
kid-skin. The Greeks probably adopted their use from th
East, for Xenophon in his *Cyropædia* mentions as a note
worthy fact that the Persians wore gloves in winter; but the
were known as early as the Homeric Age, for when Ulysse
returns after his long absence he finds his old father workin
in the garden in gloves. They must, indeed, have been mucl
used for all kinds of agricultural work. Pliny mentions then
as indispensable for harvesting esparto, which quickly tear
the unprotected flesh, and as Varro recommends that olive
should be gathered with the naked hand, gloves must commonly
have been used for that purpose. We are told that Anaxarchus
a certain gourmet in the suite of Alexander on his Asiatic

68

c. 1400

ITALIAN LADY WITH GAUNTLETS
From a miniature in the Barberini Library, Rome

xpedition, made his slaves wear gloves to knead the dough
or his bread. These things are all a matter of taste! Furthermore, the Greeks and Romans, who dipped in the dish and ate
with their fingers, wore gloves at table, both to keep their
hands clean and to preserve them from burns. Roman
" pancratiastæ," boxers and wrestlers of the arena, wore gloves
einforced with iron—to the great detriment of each other's
noses and ears.

That gloves survived the collapse of the ancient civilisation
was due to the fact that the clergy had adopted them for
liturgical purposes. The priest wore gloves at Mass, so that
he might offer the Holy Sacrifice with clean and pure hands.

69

A bishop at his consecration was given a ring, a staff and
pair of gloves, the ring as a sign that the bride of Christ wa
entrusted to his care, the staff wherewith to guide his floc
the gloves that he might do his office with clean hands. Thu
the gloves, as an essential item of clerical vesture, becam
exclusive to the bishop, and jealous watch was kept that th
lower clergy should not make use of them. The Council c
Poitiers expressly forbade even abbots to wear them. Thes
gloves were made of silk and richly embroidered on the back
usually with the cross in gold, the Agnus Dei, or some othe
Christian symbol. The gloves of William of Wykeham, Bisho
of Winchester, benefactor of New College, Oxford, are of re
silk, stitched in gold, with the monogram IHS in a glory
According to Durandus, these gloves should properly have bee
white. Pope Boniface VIII wore gloves of white silk mag
nificently embroidered and stitched with pearls, but violet an
green were also worn, and early in the fourteenth century th
clergy were forbidden to wear red gloves, or gloves striped wit
green. Luxury did not rest content with mere embroidery
when Richard de Gravesend, Bishop of London, died in 1303 h
left gloves which, besides being embroidered in gold thread
were set with enamels. This pair were valued at the time a
£5, an almost incredibly large sum, which should probably b
multiplied by twenty to obtain the value in modern pre
war money.

Gloves as part of a bishop's vestments can be traced bac
as far as the sixth century, and it is probable that the laity
began to wear them about the same time. The Anglo-Saxo
Song of Beowulf, a seventh-century work, relates how the gian
Grendel wore about his person gloves magically made from
dragon-skin; he used them as pockets. In Germany anc
Scandinavia tradition in this matter takes us back to th
eighth century and gloves are frequently mentioned as th
possession and ornament of great personages. The *Song o,
Roland*, for example, refers to them repeatedly. In the nint
century we hear that white leather is the best material fo
gloves, though it is a debatable matter whether these glove

70

MEN'S GLOVES KNITTED OF NATURAL-COLOURED SILK
Fifteenth Century

were mittens or true gloves with separate fingers. Probably the fingers were not separated till about the eleventh century. In the *Walthari-Lied* there appears to be a fairly plain reference to gloves with fingers, for Hagen mockingly advises Walther to stuff with wool the glove of the right hand (which he had lost in battle) so that he might seem to be in possession of that member.

It was not till the close of the first ten centuries of the Christian era and the beginning of the second that women began to wear gloves, an innovation which Provençal poetry ascribes to Sir Iwein. But the ladies probably needed little masculine assistance in the matter. Certainly the fashion spread very quickly, for Ulrich von Liechtenstein, who rode to the tourney dressed as a woman, felt that his masquerade as "Madame Venus" was imperfect without gloves, and the author of the *Gesta Romanorum*, a collection of popular legends, thinks it incumbent on him to warn maidens to beware lest they become the Devil's prey through accepting gloves as presents.

Gloves, whether of silk or leather, long remained very costly. A company of German merchants trading with England in the time of King Ethelred II (979-1016) had to deliver that monarch five pairs of gloves in return for the privileges he granted them. They must therefore have been something of a rarity. There is not one to be seen in the famous Bayeux Tapestry picturing the Duke of Normandy's expedition to England. They also remained expensive because kings and great lords were wont to have their gloves adorned with

71

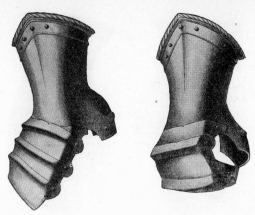

IRON GAUNTLETS, FORMING PART OF A COMPLETE SUIT OF ARMOUR
Early Sixteenth Century

precious stones. Such gloves are to be seen in effigy on the tombs of English kings, and when the graves of King Edward I at Winchester and King John at Worcester were opened, in 1774 and 1797 respectively, these monarchs' actual jewelled gloves were found. King Richard Cœur de Lion, journeying homeward from the Crusade through the territory of his enemy the Duke of Austria and therefore having every reason to remain incognito, was imprudent enough to retain his costly gloves. By these he was recognised and became a prisoner.

Gloves formed part of the coronation robes of emperors of the one-time Holy Roman Empire. A pair have been preserved and are of crimson material within and without, embroidered with a scroll pattern in gold thread, the interstices being sewn with seed-pearls, with large pearls, gems, and enamel ornaments in addition. They were probably made early in the thirteenth century for one of the Hohenstaufen Emperors by Saracen court embroiderers at Palermo. They are in Vienna to-day. A similar but less elaborate pair was lost at the close of the eighteenth century when these relics were being conveyed from Nuremberg to Vienna during the retreat before the French. This pair was of dogskin, stitched in red silk with a so-called "English" seam. At the wrist

72

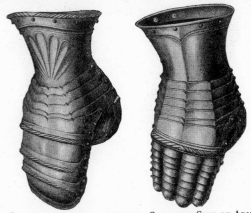

IRON GAUNTLETS FORMING PART OF A COMPLETE SUIT OF ARMOUR
Early Sixteenth Century

they had a narrow border in violet silk embroidered in a simple scroll pattern with imitation pearls. It is supposed that these dated from the thirteenth century.

Much that may perhaps be called over-decoration of the glove was retained in the case of gloves forming part of ceremonial dress even when it was no longer applied to gloves for ordinary wear. At his death in 1493, Ulrich von Freundsberg, Bishop of Trent, left one pair of gloves stitched with pearls and precious stones, and another with his monogram and arms as a prince of the Church in gold thread. In 1563, Gil Sanchez de Bazan delivered to the Spanish Treasurer various articles forming part of the Imperial insignia which Charles V had entrusted to his care, among them gold fabric gloves with a pattern worked upon them in red silk and stitched with six hundred and sixty-six globe pearls, not counting seed-pearls. Gold brocade gloves, believed to have come down from Edward the Confessor, also formed part of the English crown jewels till these were distrained in 1642 and broken up in 1649.

By the thirteenth century, gloves had become a regular part of the wardrobe of both sexes and fashion began to take charge of them. Elegant young Normans, for example, wore

73

their gloves so wide and long that once they had put them on they could do nothing at all with their hands. The gauntlet glove was the more usual shape, though effigies of noblewomen as early as 1365 occasionally show mittens. The usual material was leather, and an account for the dauphin in 1352 mentions kid, hare-skin and buckskin. There was room for extravagant expenditure in buttons, and an account of the same date, 1352, specifies gloves of dogskin covered with kid, two pair having forty-eight golden buttons and four knots of pearls. For the sport of falconry buff-leather gloves were worn (one only, not a pair) on which the hawk might perch. Henry VIII's hunting equipment at Hampton Court included seven single hawking gloves. King Henry II of England was reproached with only wearing gloves when he went hawking and never at other times!

As the use of gloves became more general they could no longer all be made in the home, and a craft began to grow up which organised itself into a guild in Perth, Scotland, as early as 1165. The earliest French guild of glove-makers dates from the year 1190. The glove-makers had not long exercised their craft when they began to make goods of inferior quality and sell them to their customers as first-rate articles. Johannes de Garlandia openly accuses them of this as early as 1220, saying that the glove-makers use every kind of skin that comes their way without discrimination. The mechanisation of the industry first made extravagance possible. In a single year (1386–7) the French King Charles VI wore out two hundred and fifty-one pairs of gloves, the Queen, Isabeau de Bavière, thirty-five pairs, and the King's brother, the Duke of Touraine, eighty pairs. By this time they had ceased to be decorated with precious stones. King Henry II of England had two pairs stitched with gems, whereas Edward IV had eighteen plain pairs in his wardrobe. Rings were sometimes worn over the glove, but sometimes the glove was slashed above the place where the ring was worn.

Gloves formed part of the fully-armed knight's equipment. These iron gauntlets, in which the thumb only was separated,

74

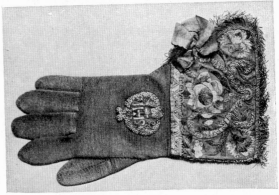

PONTIFICAL GLOVES, KNITTED AND EMBROIDERED
Sixteenth Century. National Museum, Munich

75

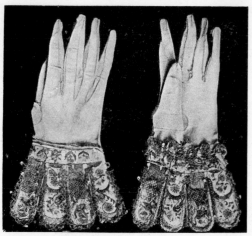

WHITE GLOVES. *Elizabethan*

were secured across the palm by iron links or strips of sheet-iron. Towards the close of the thirteenth century chain-mail gauntlets were commonly stiffened with whalebone.

The wearing of gloves was regarded as the privilege of the upper classes and even in the days of Charlemagne the peasant was reminded that he might only wear fingerless gloves. Naturally, this could not be enforced. In the *Seifried Helbling* the peasants are accused of wearing Venetian gloves, and Neidhart von Reuenthal, who has little love for the peasants, complains that they glove themselves to the elbows.

In the Middle Ages, however, the glove was something far more than a mere article of fashion; it was a symbol of the very highest significance. It must be remembered that few even of the greatest persons could write at all fluently, so that on many occasions they had to make use of signs to attest or emphasise their purpose and meaning. The glove was one such symbol. Among the Franks, the Germans, the Lombards and the Saxons the transfer of goods, real estate in particular, was confirmed by giving the assignee a glove. The bestowal of a glove also signified the granting of authority by a feudal lord to his vassal, the glove being the visible sign of investiture.

76

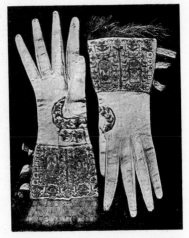

A GLOVE OF QUEEN
MARY STUART

GLOVES OF QUEEN ELIZABETH OF ENGLAND
Presented by the University of Oxford

In the *Mirror of the Saxons* it is written: "When new towns are builded a cross is to be set up in the market-place, for a sign that the public peace runs there, and there shall be hung thereon the King's glove, for a sign that it is the King's will." The Emperor conferred upon towns the right of holding market by sending them his glove. In all these instances the glove stood for a symbol of unbreakable promise and had all the value of a chartered and sealed covenant. Conversely, the glove was also the pledge that the vassal had to deliver to his feudal overlord. When the city of Königsberg did homage to the Duke of Prussia it presented him with a left-hand glove and three hundred pence. The monastery of Arnsberg near Giessen was bound to deliver gloves to the Landgrave of Hesse. In these cases the glove was a symbol of submission. This symbolic method of dealing persisted in the Holy Roman Empire till its downfall. Goethe speaks in *Wahrheit und Dichtung* of the measure of awe with which he used to see his grandfather Textor put on the gloves which had yearly to be paid by dependant municipalities to the city of Frankfort-on-Main. When, on the other hand, any ill-doer was put under

77

the interdict the monarch, or his judge, would cast away the defaulter's glove, therewith declaring the criminal outlawed and his goods confiscate. Again, when the king dispatched a messenger on important business he accredited him by giving him a staff with his glove attached.

In the world of chivalry the glove had a great part to play. If a knight wished to challenge another he struck him with his glove, an insult necessitating a combat to the death. If he could not strike him he would throw down his glove as a challenge. When a combat between two knights was arranged both gave their gloves as pledges that they would not fail to appear at the time and place appointed. Conradin von Hohenstaufen, standing on the very scaffold, threw his glove down amidst the throng so that it might be carried to his kin as a token of his cause and his claims. It was taken up by Heinrich Truchsess von Waldburg and carried to King Peter of Aragon, who afterwards succeeeded in taking possession of Sicily and had himself crowned king in Palermo.

A part of the ceremonial at the coronation of the Kings of England, retained down to the nineteenth century, was the throwing down of a glove as a challenge to anyone who disputed the King's right to reign. It is said that at the coronation of George III in Westminster Abbey the glove was taken up and conveyed to Charles Edward Stuart, the Pretender, who did not, however, claim his rights. The symbolic ceremony was enacted for the last time at the coronation of George IV. Charles I, at his execution, gave away the gloves he was wearing, and in the same way Lady Jane Grey and Mary Stuart gave their gloves on the scaffold as a last pledge. Gloves used at ordeals were of iron, made red hot and placed upon the prisoners hands after blessing by the priest.

Although the lady's glove had not quite so much significance attached to it as the knight's, yet it was by no means an object of indifference. When a lady gave her glove to a man it was a token that he might expect the final proof of her favour. Donna Anna de Mendoza set her suitor a severe test when she let her glove fall among the lions in the arena before the

78

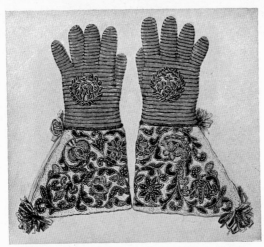

CEREMONIAL GLOVES.   KING LOUIS XIII OF FRANCE

assembled court of King Juan III of Castile; but as we know from the ballads of Schiller and Robert Browning the incident ended in some humiliation to herself, for the knight threw the recovered glove in the lady's face, saying he would never ask thanks of her.   Ordinarily, of course, the fair were content to surrender their gloves to their admirers under milder conditions.   Like other articles of their ladies' attire (the shift itself not excluded!), knights wore their gloves in their helms in tourney or battle.   Such attentions actually continued to be paid when the days of chivalric woman-worship were long past.   Clifford, Earl of Cumberland, wore the bediamonded glove of Elizabeth, the Virgin Queen, in his hat.   When the Winter King had lost Bohemia and he and his consort wandered homeless, Prince Christian of Brunswick, constituting himself his cousin's knight, fastened one of her gloves to his helmet and swore he would not give it her again till he entered Prague victorious at her side; she never got it back.

Naturally enough, etiquette concerned itself with the glove, as with the hat.   It was not permissible to appear with covered head in all places and on all occasions, and similarly there

79

were circumstances when gloves might not be worn. The *Mirror of the Saxons* lays it down that judges may not wear gloves when exercising their office. Again, a man might not appear gloved before the king, and pious people would not wear gloves in church. Gloves were laid aside on occasions of deep mourning. To offer another a gloved hand was an unpardonable breach of good manners. If a gentleman were escorting a lady he wore gloves, but if dancing with her he took them off. To dance without gloves was a special refinement of the Court. Country bumpkins were laughed at because they imitated gentlemen by wearing gloves and yet knew so little of etiquette as to put them on for dances.

Many of these customs struck deep root in court ceremonial. To offer or to take anything with gloves on was the grossest blunder of which a well-bred man could be guilty. When Philip Hainhofer was received by the Duchess of Bavaria in Munich in 1611 she drew off her gloves each time they met, a fact which he does not fail to notice as a proof of her great courtesy. This may have been the reason why gentlemen in the fifteenth century usually carried their gloves stuck in their belts, where they were safe at least from giving offence. If one may trust the pictures, gloves were usually carried in the hand in the sixteenth century. Portraits both of men and women seldom show them as wearing more than one glove. One may perhaps venture a guess why. Both sexes wore gloves of the same cut and both wore them much too big. If we may judge by the pictures, their fit left everything to be desired. Queen Elizabeth of England, therefore, who was very vain of her beautiful hands, when giving audience would keep on drawing her gloves on and off. The gloves preserved in certain English collections and ascribed to Elizabeth or to her rival Mary Stuart are of dimensions which certainly did not correspond very accurately to those of the hands of their fair possessors. At least, one hopes not!

The earlier gloves were all either of leather or of fabric that required to be hand-sewn, but about the end of the fifteenth and beginning of the sixteenth century the woven glove came

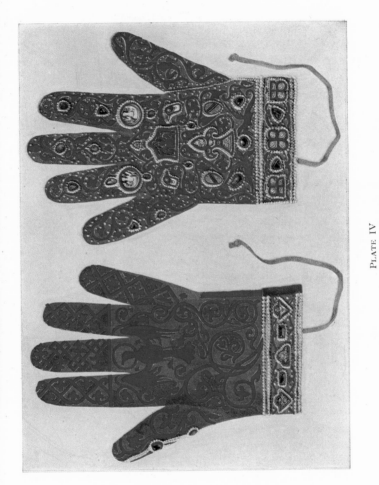

PLATE IV

CORONATION GLOVES OF THE GERMAN EMPERORS

12th Century. *Imperial Treasury, Vienna.*

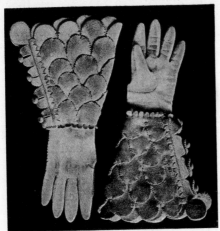

GAUNTLETS. *Seventeenth Century*

n, shortly followed by the knitted glove. These were made in he Netherlands and were frequently of silk. Though they had he advantage over the sewn gloves of being elastic, they never appear to have attained the same popularity in the fashionable world. The leather glove, ending in a long and wide gauntlet cuff, was the favourite. This cuff was richly decorated. Queen Elizabeth's gloves in the Bodleian Library are of white leather, stitched in gold; those of Mary Stuart are worked in silver thread and coloured silks. Horace Walpole possessed a pair of gloves belonging to King James I made of brown leather, with the cuffs stitched in red silk and gold thread. Articles of this sort were dear. A pair presented to Queen Elizabeth by the University of Cambridge in 1578 cost sixty shillings, as much as King Edward VI had paid for six pairs of plain sporting gloves.

The perfuming of gloves was a very old custom and had been practised in France from the close of the thirteenth century, though it did not become an important matter till the six-teenth, when the Spanish glove became fashionable, bringing with it the peculiar odour which became proverbial. All through the sixteenth century Spanish gloves were in the highest

G

degree articles of luxury. In 1523 a joust took place at th
court of the Emperor Charles V at which the first prize con
sisted of forty pairs of perfumed Spanish gloves, valued a
two hundred ducats. In a list of jewels and valuables a
Pressburg Castle in 1527 a box with four pairs of perfumed
gloves is not forgotten. In an inventory of the effects of Anna
"Queen of the Romans," who died in 1547, there is mentioned
a chest of "good costly Spanish gloves," fourteen pairs being
actually Spanish, and forty-two pairs Italian. The widower
the future Emperor Maximilian II, had this store distributed
among his six daughters, three pairs to each princess and the
remainder for himself. In 1544 a certain lady of rank gave
Princess Mary of England a little chest containing ten pairs
of Spanish gloves, and the princess gave the bearer thirty
shillings. The Archduke Ferdinand of Tyrol, who married
Philippine Welser, had in his wardrobe in 1569 thirteen pairs
of black perfumed gloves and six pairs of white Spanish gloves,
one pair with crystal fastenings. In 1565 the Duchess of
Ferrara, an archduchess of Austria, left a dozen pairs of Spanish
gloves, and Andreas Masius conscientiously notes that in 1566
he was presented by Anton de Tassis of Antwerp with three
pairs of perfumed Spanish gloves. The effects of Queen
Elizabeth of France, widow of Charles III, who died in 1593,
included three pairs of white and two pairs of black Spanish
perfumed gloves. Only a king could have made such a present
as Philip III gave his bride, the Archduchess Margaret, in 1599
on her arrival in Barcelona, when he sent her two hundred
pairs of gloves. When Louise de Lorraine, widow of Henry III,
died in 1601 she left thirteen pairs of perfumed gloves.

These articles of attire, so costly in themselves, were rendered
even more so by the buttons with which they were furnished.
In 1577, Queen Elizabeth of England received from Lady Grey
two pairs of Spanish gloves with four dozen gold buttons, a
real pearl in each, and the following year Lady Mary Sidney
presented her with a pair with two dozen buttons in gold, each
set with a diamond. Antonio Perez, Philip's II's traitorous
Secretary-of-State, gained influential friends of both sexes

PORTRAIT OF SIR — SHEFFIELD

during his exile in England and France by his gifts of Spanish
gloves. He accompanied his present to Lady Knolles with
the assurance that the gloves were made from the skin of the
most faithful of hounds, and on another occasion he assured
Lady Rich that he would willingly let himself be flayed to make
her a pair of gloves from his skin. Perhaps he was indeed
"souple comme un gant d'Espagne," as the proverb went then
in France.

Gloves were always a welcome gift. The English Chancellor,
Sir Thomas More, received from a lady, who was grateful for
having won a case tried before him, a pair of gloves which,
she said, she had made with her own hands and which were

83

filled with gold pieces. He sent back the money, but gallantl
kept the gloves. At court festivities in Ferrara the Duke alway
presented the ladies invited with perfumed gloves, and i
England the custom of presenting gloves as new-year's gift
became so general that, when in the sixteenth century th
gloves came to be replaced by money, the money gift retaine
the name of "glove money."

In an age when consciences were none too tender as to th
means employed to an end, the dressing of leather with stron
smelling perfumes was enough to make people fear the possi
bility of being poisoned by means of gloves. As early as 1066
Conan, Duke of Brittany, was reputed to have been murdere
by a pair of poisoned gloves, and it was said at the time, and i
still asserted to-day, that Jeanne d'Albret, mother of Henry IV
was poisoned by means of a pair of gloves at the French Court
Whether it would be actually possible to cause death by such
a method is uncertain, but there is no doubt that specially
prepared gloves could cause skin diseases. Law cases of the
kind were heard in England as late as the nineteenth century
and such attempts are said to have been made on Adelina
Patti.

In the sixteenth century the wearing of gloves became
fairly general. Effeminate fops, such as Henry III of France
and his minions, even wore gloves at night, changing them
by day for gloves slashed to show the red silk lining. But
even gentlemen who were very far from exaggerated dandyism
of this kind became much addicted to them, and Montaigne, in
his third book of *Essays*, writes that he could as ill do without
his gloves as without his hands.

The very conscientiousness with which every pair of gloves
is noted down in the inventories of princely houses shows the
importance which was attached to those articles. The same
fact is made plain in wills, where gloves are disposed of as
objects of great value. In 1578, the Emperor Maximilian II
left the Archduke Albert a pair of "white otter-skin gloves"
and the Archduke Ernest two pairs of velvet gloves. When
the Archduke Ferdinand of Tyrol died in 1596 Cardinal Andreas

sked that "men's gloves rom Mantua and the Netherlands" should be llotted to him from his father's effects.

The mention of Mantuan gloves brings us to the fact that Spain had strong competition to contend with in the manufacture of this article. Edward de Vere, Earl of Oxford, brought Queen Elizabeth perfumed gloves from Italy, and shortly afterwards they began to be made on the hither side of both

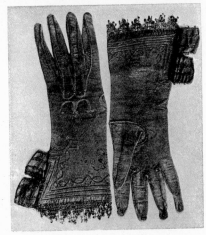

GLOVES OF KING CHARLES I OF ENGLAND

Alps and Pyrenees. The very fastidious soon asserted that to get gloves of the very first quality, the leather should come from Spain, should be cut out in France and sewn in England. In France a kind that was greatly prized came from Vendôme and was said to be so fine that a pair of these leather gloves could be packed in a nut-shell. In Limerick, Ireland, gloves were made of the skins of unborn calves and were known as "Limericks" after the place of their origin. Hans Jacob von Breuning, who was sent to England in 1595 as the ambassador of the Duke of Würtemburg, took his master back three pairs of English gloves from London. Germany, too, bestirred itself. Philip Hainhofer, writing in his travel journal at Innsbruck in 1628, says: "They make here fine and delicate gloves, neatly sewn, which are distributed far and wide." The repute of the Italian glove industry continued to increase at the expense of that of Spain. Anne of Austria ordered her gloves by the dozen in Naples, and in 1649, Monsieur de Chanteloup, in Paris, commissioned the painter Poussin, in Rome, to get him a dozen pairs there. In Germany, too, Italian gloves were prized and Abraham à Santa Clara cried in one of his famous moral

85

LADIES' GLOVES. *Seventeenth Century*

sermons: "What boots it that a man wear a pair of sweet-scented Roman gloves, when there are sharp scratching claws within?" During his stay in London Count Grammont sent every week to Paris to procure gloves.

As regards shape, the gauntlet glove remained in favour, the wide cuff being trimmed with embroidery, and later also (as Cromwell, for instance, seems to have liked them), with silken fringes. When James I and his Queen paid their first visit to Oxford in 1605 the University presented the royal couple with two pairs of leather gloves with gold fringes and real pearls as fastenings. This little attention cost the University twelve pounds sterling. In 1622 the University of Cambridge did honour to the Lord Chancellor with somewhat similar gloves, less elaborately trimmed and costing only forty-four shillings the pair. With special garments, such as the costumes worn at masques, gloves were worn to match. The Elector John George I of Saxony had a suit of parrot-green atlas, embroidered all over in silver and coloured silks, with gloves of the same material, similarly embroidered and having cuffs of yellow atlas worked in coloured silk. The glove with the wide gauntlet cuff gave rise to all sorts of trick gloves, gloves which the recipient could not draw on his hand, etc. Thus, in the trick cabinet purchased from Philip Hainhofer by the Archduke of Innsbruck for presentation to his son-in-law the Grand Duke of Tuscany, Hainhofer put, among other things,

86

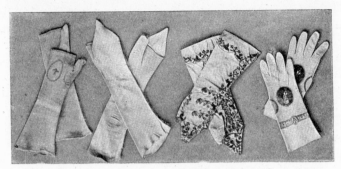

LADIES' MITTENS OF WHITE ATLAS, THE EMBROIDERED PAIR OF THE
ROCOCO PERIOD, THE OTHERS OF THE EMPIRE PERIOD; AND A MAN'S
GLOVES OF THE LATE EIGHTEENTH CENTURY

"a pair of trick surprise gloves of buckskin." Such jests were
very popular then, and people gave each other pistols that
would not fire, set drinking cups before their guests that
inevitably spilled liquor over them, and indulged in all sorts
of similar practical jokes.

The consumption of gloves increased apace. Prince Henry
of Wales, elder brother of the future King Charles I, at fourteen
years of age used in a single year thirty-one pairs of perfumed,
silver- and gold-laced and otherwise decorated gloves. An
inventory of the Treasury in Vienna for 1619 mentions forty-
five pairs of perfumed, and eight dozen pairs of Spanish
gloves. A veritable mania for gloves must have taken possession of the Archduke Charles, Grand-Master of the Teutonic
Order, who died in 1626, reminding one of that later Prince
of Prussia who went for the day to Dessau to attend a funeral
and, so it is said, deemed it indispensable to take with him
twenty-four straw hats and eighty pairs of boots! Archduke
Charles was no less well provided with gloves. There were
found among his effects seventy-nine pairs of Spanish gloves,
another ten pairs embroidered in gold and silver and valued
at ten reichstaler the pair, seven pairs embroidered and worth
eighteen reichstaler a pair, seven pairs more at eight reichstaler,
one pair, stitched with black beads, at five reichstaler; and let
it be remembered that these sums must be multiplied by five

87

at least to estimate their value in pre-war money, also that the purchasing power of money in those days was probably higher out of all proportion. However, the Grand-Master of the Teutonic Order's achievement pales before that of a lady. When Anne of Austria closed her eyes for ever in 1666 she was found to have left three hundred pairs of gloves. As a native of Spain she had purchased most of them in that country.

Towards the end of the seventeenth century the trimming of gloves became less elaborate. The Archduke Leopold William, the renowned collector from whose galleries are derived the best part of the valuable pictures in the Court Museum, Vienna, left gaily embroidered gloves, gloves with golden fringes or embroidered in gold and silver thread, and black leather gloves embroidered in gold, but the taste for these had already passed out of fashion. After centuries of luxurious adornment of the glove there followed a century which was very restrained in this respect. Not only did fringes, embroideries and gems disappear, but gentlemen ceased to wear gloves at all. Fashion largely contributed to this, for she decked out the dandy in lace cuffs of such length that the hand was completely covered and needed no other protection. In England in the reigns of George I and George II decorum demanded that at a ball a gentleman should put on a fresh pair of gloves for each dance, but in France this custom too was dropped. The Duchesse d'Abrantès recollected that in her youth, which fell in the last decade of the eighteenth century, a gentleman never wore gloves except when riding or hunting, and even then, should he forget to draw off his gloves at the very moment of dismounting from his horse, they became the perquisites of the huntsman or groom who might demand them of him.

Officers, however, wore light wash-leather gloves, a circumstance which was to prove fatal to Prince Leopold of Brunswick. He was with the garrison at Frankfort-on-Oder and on the occasion of a great flood was assisting in the rescue of the threatened inhabitants when his boat overturned; the Prince fell into the water, and his soaked gloves became so slippery that they defeated all his efforts to obtain a hold on the boat;

LADY'S GLOVES OF WHITE ATLAS, EMBROIDERED, EIGHTEENTH CENTURY, AND HUNTING GLOVE OF THE SEVENTEENTH CENTURY

he groping hands slipped again and again and he sank and as drowned.

Gloves were, however, retained by ladies, who wore elbow-ength sleeves during most of the century. Caraccioli, an talian domiciled in Paris who wrote on matters of fashion 1 the middle of the century, went so far as to say that a dy *must* change her gloves from four to five times a day. hey were very strongly perfumed with such scents as gum enjamin, ambergris, musk and oil of jasmine, orange-flowers nd lemon-flowers. Possibly this was necesary owing to certain rocesses in manufacture. The glacé kid gloves made in Ber-n, for example, had, according to Krünitz, a very unpleasant dour, so that French and Italian gloves were greatly preferred. he Infanta Isabella of Parma, the first wife of Joseph II, eceived for her trousseau in 1760 twelve dozen pairs of glacé id gloves from Turin, while the trousseau prepared at the rench court for the Dauphine Marie Antoinette contained loves to the value of 5,778 francs.

The old custom, dating from medieval times, that nothing night be handed to an exalted personage save with hands ngloved, remained in force. Madame Campan, waiting-oman to Marie Antoinette, tells a very amusing story which hows how inconvenient this custom must often have been.)ne evening, as the Queen was standing quite unclothed and vas about to put on the chemise which the waiting-woman was anding her, a lady of the court entered and claimed the office

her privilege. She had, however, first to remove her glov
and had scarcely done so when a princess arrived who too
precedence in the matter. The business of removing glov
was repeated when a princess of the blood appeared to who
the privilege passed, so that all the while these ladies we
removing their gloves and making ceremony with the chemi
the Queen was forced to stand naked, waiting for her visito
to come to the point of actually handing her her garment!

At the court of the first Napoleon gloves were once mo
worn, but fashion went to no extravagant lengths in the
trimming. Even the gloves made for the coronation of Nap
leon and Josephine in 1804 cost only thirty-three francs a pa
and can only have been very modestly embroidered. The fou
pairs of gold-embroidered gloves the Emperor purchased f
his marriage with Marie Louise in 1810 cost altogether only 14
francs. Napoleon loved to wear very soft leather. He had
strikingly small hand of which he was extremely vain. Whe
the officers of his suite wished to offer him a little delica
flattery they would pretend to accidentally pick up and t
to put on one of his gloves, purely for the sake of displayir
well-simulated astonishment when it appeared that not o
of them could get into them. He used a great many pai
each year, two hundred and thirty pairs of cream-coloure
gloves in 1806 besides the forty-two pairs of fur-lined glov
which he bought at the cost of 865 francs in December of th
year. During the Hundred Days, sixty pairs sufficed hir
and he must have gone very short of them as an exile on S
Helena. Only six pairs were found at his death.

The eighteenth century, which neglected gloves, wa
followed by a century which brought them once more in
favour. Even gentlemen took to wearing them again. Bea
Brummel, the famous English dandy, said that the perfe
glove must be the work of three separate workmen, one to c
the hand, a second the fingers and a third the thumb. I
1839, as Count d'Orsay wrote from London, an Englis
gentleman needed six different pairs of gloves daily. Ecce
tricities, however, such as the future Lord Beaconsfield pe

mitted himself when, as young Mr. Disraeli, he wanted at all
costs to make a splash in Paris and wore white glacé kid gloves
with long black silk fringes, obtained no following.

The ladies, who had never abandoned gloves, now took to
wearing them almost continuously. In Paris in 1823 they
wore them at meals and even when playing the harp and
clavier. There was little variation in cut or trimming and
change of fashion was chiefly confined to colour. For a time
yellow was so very much the mode that "gant jaune" became
the slang phrase for "dandy" in Paris. There were frequent
changes in the length of ladies' gloves; according to fashion's

UNIFORM GLOVE OF AN
OFFICER OF THE PARIS
MILITIA (1795)

whims they might be wrist-length
elbow-length or almost shoulder-length
In the 'seventies, when Sarah Bern
hardt, who had thin and ugly arms
was at the height of her fame, she
introduced a fashion for gloves so long
that they formed innumerable wrinkle
up the arm. For a time black glove
were worn with light dresses, the
fashion repented and returned to whit
gloves. Kid gloves and softer suèd
alternated; the stitched seams on th
backs were sometimes broad and some
times narrow, sometimes of a contrast
ing shade, sometimes matching th
tone of the glove. It would be a
endless and wearisome task to follow
all the minor changes dictated b
fashion and it is enough to note tha
variations were frequent.

Throughout the century, in any case, gloves of some kind
were indispensable for completing the elegant woman's toilet
and no lady would have ventured to show herself in the stree
or in society without them. In affairs of the heart, too, the
played their part. Even though no knight carried his lady'
glove in his helm, many a one in the blissful folly of yout
carried it next his heart. Max Klinger wrote one of his mos
ingenious works round the incident of the finding of a glov
lost by a lady on a roller-skating rink. The sketch, whic
appeared in 1878, tells in ten pages how the gentleman wh
found and kept the glove became the victim through thi
apparently harmless object of an unreal passion and romanti
dreams. The manner in which, in this dream life, the shape
material and perfume of the glove translate themselves int
all sorts of strange phenomena and events is most poeticall
and pertinently described. No such inspiration could hav
occurred to the artist to-day, for since ladies hardly wea

92

loves at all they naturally cannot lose them! Women have
ecome masculine; and a sunburned tint, formerly considered
unbecoming, is thought beautiful to-day—or at least a guarantee
f health. Since white hands are no longer fashionable, what
s the use of gloves? How long will they survive?

GLOVES OF QUEEN ANNE OF ENGLAND,
LEFT BY HER IN OXFORD IN 1702

Hans Holbein
MAGISTRATE WITH WALKING-STICK
From the "Dance of Death"

CHAPTER IV

WALKING-STICKS

THE stick is the earliest implement in the history of huma
culture. Primitive man, wishing to reinforce the natura
strength of his arm, either for attack or defence, would naturall
seize upon a stick. Thus it became the first weapon, and nex
by a natural transition, the earliest symbol of sovereignty, a
emblem of strength, dignity and power. It seems almos
unnecessary to pursue so self-evident an argument in an
detail.

Kings and priests, dividing as they did all authority betwee
them, must therefore have been the first to bear the staff a
a token of their exalted position. At Persepolis there a1
Persian bas-reliefs showing the king enthroned and holding i
his right hand a long staff with a round knob at one enc
Similarly the Greeks represented their supreme gods—Zeu
with the staff, Poseidon with the trident, Hermes with th

Right and Left: KNOBS OF WALKING-STICKS SET WITH DIAMONDS (*designed by Mondon, Paris, c.* 1740). *Centre:* DESIGNS FOR THE KNOBS OF WALKING-STICKS
J. J. Baumgartner, Augsburg, 1725

duceus and Dionysus with the thyrsus. These divine
signia passed over to the priesthood, as though in some
anner enduing it with the supposed powers inherent in them.
the Old Testament Jehovah is represented as showing forth
s will through Aaron's staff, and the story in the seventeenth
apter of the Book of Numbers of the rod that budded was
ken by early Christians as signifying the general call of the
hole priesthood to the Lord's service.

The tradition which places the staff in the form of the
eptre in the hand of kings is, we may be sure, of remote
ntiquity, as old as the earliest beginnings of human history;
ut it has since been allotted to all who exercise authority,
ot only as kings and priests, but also as judges, as military
mmanders, as ambassadors and, significantly, as sorcerers,
hom indeed one can scarcely picture apart from the magic
and in which a great part of their power resided! Down
the eighteenth century a fairy or sorceress was invariably

95

recognisable on the French stage by the little wand she carrie in her hand. To the upper ranks of society the staff was there fore a symbol, while to the lower it was and continued to t an indispensable implement of daily use. Shepherds, tille. of the soil, and travellers regularly carried a staff which wa in a manner, part of their stock-in-trade. It was not withou profound significance that the Greek myth made Prometheu conceal in his pilgrim's staff the divine fire which he had stole from the gods that he might bring blessings to men.

The Middle Ages appear to have thought one sceptre ii sufficient and gave the king a second, the so-called "Hand (Justice." The sceptre proper was still carried in the rigl hand and the staff, surmounted by a hand in the attitude (blessing, was placed in the left. In France this custom dat from the days of Hugh Capet. When the treasures of tl Abbey of St. Denis were shown to the Emperor Charles V i 1539, his attention was drawn to such a "main de justice which was supposed to be made from the horn of a unicor English kings adopted the custom, and Richard Cœur de Lio who was twice crowned (in 1188 and again in 1194), was c each occasion invested with both sceptres. Napoleon, wl liked to think himself the direct successor of Charlemagne an wished to proclaim it by a visible sign, caused a "Hand of Ju tice" to be made for his coronation as King of Italy in Mila in 1804; the staff is gilt bronze and the hand itself is ivor it cost 2,800 francs.

The Church, the great rival of the civil power, provided i highest officials also with this staff symbolic of authority. Fro: the dawn of the Middle Ages the pastoral staff was an emble. of the bishop's dignity and by the sixth century it plain stood for his authority as shepherd of the flock. The id took such deep root that this staff of office eventually becam the symbol of the cathedral itself. In the days of the Ca lovingians and the Ottos, the pastoral staff was brought to tl king on the death of a bishop, and the king delivered it to tl new bishop on his election with the words "Accipe ecclesiam The oldest form of the pastoral staff is long and crook-handle

96

"FINE WALKING-STICKS!" PARIS STREET-
HAWKER (*c.* 1760)

he shaft of wood, the crook of ivory, either plain or carved
nd sometimes containing a reliquary. The episcopal staff
f St. Rupert in the monastery of St. Peter at Salzburg is of
his shape, as is also that of St. Heribert at Deutz. After the
welfth century the true crook-handled staff ceased to be used
1 the Western Church and the pastoral staff thenceforward
as made with a knob near the top, above which it took a
ook-like bend. The symbol-loving mind of the age sought
o invest the new form with deep meaning. According to
Ionorius of Autun, the hook signified that the bishop drew
ne faithful to himself; the sharp point, with which the staff
as shod, that he spurred on the lukewarm to greater effort.

Pastoral staffs were often of very rich workmanship, the
haft perhaps of wood, the knob of crystal and the hook above,
vhich frequently ended in the form of a dragon's head, of

H   97

copper-gilt, bronze or ivory; they were sometimes ornamente
with pictures showing Christ's conflict with the Evil One, th
Church's victory over the devil, and kindred subjects. Fro
the thirteenth century onwards some specimens exist mac
entirely of ivory. Gothic art overcharged the handle (if suc
it may still be called) with a wealth of ornament. The for
was frequently quite architectural, the knob made like a tin
chapel, the hook bent into an almost complete circle surroun
ing like a frame small figures and reliefs, and the materia
used were precious metals.

A third form of the pastoral staff was that of the crozie
which was carried only by archbishops as a mark of the
greater dignity. Pope Alexander II (1061-73), howeve
granted the Bishop of Halberstadt the right to carry th
crozier as a token of special favour.

The pastoral staff was also used by abbots and abbesse
as an emblem of authority. Abbots, like those of Fuld
Einsiedeln and Kempten, who were also Princes of the Hol
Roman Empire, bore the pastoral staff side by side with th
sword in their escutcheons. There was no distinction in th
form of the staff as borne by the bishop or the abbot, exce
that the abbot had a small napkin attached to his and carrie
the staff with the crook towards the shoulder, while the bisho
carried it with the crook turned outwards.

In various forms the staff also appertained to lesser office
of the church, such as precentors, servers and heads of fr
ternities, and to pilgrims. The cathedral treasury at Cologn
contains a silver-plated staff for the precentor, dating from th
year 1178, which terminates in a trident, and similar staf
are to be found in the church treasuries at Aix, Hildeshein
Canabruck and elsewhere. To this day in the ancient cathedra
of Spain the sacristans may be seen clad in bright red sil
robes reaching to the ground, bearing in their hands lon
silver staffs, like sceptres, which the people of the countr
irreverently call *azota perros* (dog-whips)!

Pilgrim's staffs were far simpler, often mere walking-sticks
painted with the picture of the saint to whom pilgrimage wa

98

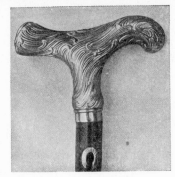

WALKING-STICK CROOKS FROM FREDERICK THE GREAT'S COLLECTION
Hohenzollern Museum, Berlin

eing made. Here and there, however, a costly specimen has
ome down, probably made for the pleasure of some person of
ank. In the Ole Olsen collection in Copenhagen is a valuable
oilgrim's staff, eighty-seven centimetres in length, and made
hroughout in ivory. It is engraved all over with pictures of
iermits and anchoresses, and may be of Spanish origin. The
one-time Bourgeois collection at Cologne, now dispersed by
ale, contained an ebony staff with a head of olive-wood, in
ront of which was a reliquary, opened and closed by a little
loor showing the form of a Virgin and Child in high relief;
ι cross of mother-of-pearl was inlaid. In the former Imperial
Treasury, Vienna, may be seen a pilgrim's staff made of cane,
overed with religious pictures; the head, the ferrule, and the
ιoops which surround the staff are of silver filigree set with
ιmethysts and almandines. The specimen dates from the
eighteenth century and was perhaps only used for those mas-
querades, then so popular, in which pilgrims of both sexes took
oart in couples. In 1750 the Imperial Treasury in Vienna
ontained a pilgrim's staff in brown wood with a round gold
knob from which a gold band spread and wound down the
staff, bearing an inscription of the genealogy of the House of
Hesse from the days of St. Elizabeth. It was a votive offering
made by the Landgrave George III of Hesse-Darmstadt (1632-
76) to his ancestress, St. Elizabeth.

99

In medieval times the judge bore a staff in the exercise of his office. Hans Holbein has portrayed one such in his *Dance of Death*. When the Reichskammergericht, the Supreme Imperial Court, was instituted in 1495 and the Emperor Maximilian appointed Count Eitelfriedrich von Hohenzollern its president, the delivery of a staff formed part of the ceremony of inauguration. This staff of the Supreme Imperial Court is made of rosewood with a simple white bone ring at one end. It was formerly kept at Wetzlar, but in 183 was transferred to the Imperial Treasury, Vienna. Subordinate executant officers of justice, tipstaffs, provosts, and similar officials also carried a staff, but carried it as weapon. In Germany, these staffs were euphemistically called "Vergleicher," that is "reconcilers," for when kind words and good reasons failed, the officers of the court would beat refractory persons about the ears until they were fully convinced! City police, gate-keepers, watchmen and officials of all sorts retained the staff as a sign of office well into the nineteenth century. In Frankfort-on-Main the night watchman was distinguished by a mighty oaken club, nicknamed the "Morgenstern," or morning star. At one time it used to be surmounted by a six-sided lantern in which a light burned, but later this was replaced by a thick wooden knob, bearing on each of its four faces the arms of Frankfort. Though apparently a most formidable weapon this staff served a peaceable purpose for it was passed from hand to hand among the watchmen and through the night till every quarter of the city was patrolled.

The high offices of marshal, lord high steward and seneschal were also signalised by the staff. In these cases it was symbolic of course, but also served practical ends. When pages became too cheeky and unmannerly the steward could, no doubt correct them with his staff of office, though the ceremonial staffs of a later day were much too precious and curiously made to be used with vigour in this manner.

The staff of a Polish Lord Chamberlain, preserved in the Green Vault, the famous Dresden museum, is set with precious stones, and the Austrian "Archducal Hereditary Chief

WALKING-STICK CROOKS FROM FREDERICK THE GREAT'S COLLECTION
Hohenzollern Museum, Berlin

Master-of-the-Horse" carried as the emblem of his office a
staff of Bengal cane with a silver knob and a red and white
strap with tassels. At the coronation of the Emperor
Ferdinand I in Milan in 1838, the "Hereditary Chief Master-
of-the-Horse of Lombardy-Venetia" officiated with a black
staff, bearing the arms and monogram of the Emperor in gold.
During the eighteenth century the long ceremonial wands of
the higher court officials began to go out of fashion and
were retained chiefly at the lesser European courts. Prince
Khevenhiller, who accompanied the Emperor Francis I and
his son on a visit to Frankfort-on-Main in 1764, writes of their
entertainment by the Margrave of Ansbach at Crailsheim and
says: "An Over- and an Under-Marshal always waited upon
us at table carrying long staffs, to the no small amusement of
the young gentlemen of our suite," showing that the actual use
of the staff can no longer have been customary at the Imperial
Court in Vienna.

The heralds who officiated at tournaments carried staffs
as emblems of office. In the Historical Museum in Dresden
are deposited two such herald's staffs of carved and painted
wood, made in Augsburg about 1450. The Royal Treasury of
Bavaria contains a herald's staff of the Order of St. Hubert,
made of green lacquered wood encased in silver gilt. It bears
a small badge in porcelain, and the whole dates from 1708.

When the miners' guilds engaged in solemn processions, one of their number carried a ceremonial staff, which was known as the "Bergmannsparthe" or miner's club. Baron Charles Rolas de Rosey of Dresden possessed two of these curious articles Both are hatchet-shaped with prismatic points, the hafts being of pear-wood, ornamented with ivory plaques of various sizes with portraits of the Electors of Saxony, a crucifix, and other pictures engraved upon them; they date from 1681 and 1686

The fact that the staff was originally a weapon was never altogether lost sight of in the "pusikan," or "buzogany," of the princes of Transylvania, which, once a club, degenerated in course of time into a mere ceremonial emblem carried upon the shoulder. This staff was made of wood encased in velvet and had a thick knob at the upper end. Numerous wars brought many fine specimens into Viennese collections, among them one constructed of various sorts of jasper and agate set in silver-gilt, and others in which a diamond-mesh net of gold filigree work, set with rubies and sapphires, encloses a crystal knob When the Rolas du Rosey Collection came under the hammer in 1863 one specimen was sold which had a large, almost spherical, knob of bronze; it bore four grotesque masks surrounded by a trefoil design and gadrooned borders and was crowned by four busts in high relief.

Formerly used as a weapon, the "pusikan" had long been merely a symbol of armed force and, as such, what we should call a "field-marshal's baton" in the hand of the supreme military authority. This piece of military equipment appears to be no older than the sixteenth century. The field-marshal's baton is first seen in the form of a long staff, without differentiation of top and bottom, in the hands of Spaniards of exalted rank. Anthonis Mor painted it in the hand of King Philip II, the Duke of Alva and others, and as it may also be seen in portraits of William of Orange and Don John of Austria everything points to a Spanish origin for this emblem.

Such a staff was certainly used by the Emperor Charles V, for when campaigning in 1543 he was so transported with rage by the phlegm with which a certain Swabian carter's man addressed himself to the transport of a piece of ordnance that he gave the fellow several blows with his staff. The Swabian, however, not recognising the Emperor, who was plainly dressed, in his assailant, returned blow for blow with his whip, and, although he lost his nose for his offence, he was able to boast up and down the land for many a year that he had belaboured His Imperial Majesty.

All such antique marshal's batons as have survived, date back no further than the sixteenth century. In the Rosenborg, Copenhagen, is preserved King Frederick II of Denmark's marshal's baton, made of wood with pictures of the Kronborg and hunting scenes in metal inlay, beneath which appear the King's monogram and the initial letters of his device, MHZGA. TIW, "Meine Hoffnung zu Gott allein. Treue ist Wildbret." When the Grand Master of the Teutonic Order, the Archduke Charles, died in 1626 he left amongst his effects his marshal's baton of cane plated with gold at either end and set with turquoises and rubies. It was valued at eighteen ducats. The Dresden History Museum contains the batons of Tilly and of Count Pappenheim, who was mortally wounded at Lützen. Tilly's baton must have been lost by him at the, to him, fatal battle of Breitenfeld, for it was picked up on the field; the staff is covered with overlapping plates of mother-of-pearl, and has a massive gold ornament, gaily enamelled; one of the two knobs bears the arms of the Bohemian chancellor, Count Wilhelm Slawata, who probably presented the baton to Tilly. The Imperial Treasury, Vienna, contained in 1750 the Emperor Ferdinand III's baton, of spirally-turned ivory with a gold enamelled portrait medallion set with ninety-three rubies; it also served its possessor as a field-glass. This baton was a gift from the Empress Marie Eleonore to her husband. At his death in 1660 the Archduke Leopold William left six marshal's batons in tortoiseshell and bamboo, some ornamented with gold and some with silver, and one of ivory mounted in gold and set with diamonds. Kara Mustapha, who laid siege to Vienna, possessed a baton made of agate and chalcedony, the gold mounting set with turquoises. King

Christian V of Denmark's baton had gold knobs set with diamonds at either end. In the Court Museum, Vienna, is a marshal's baton of the period, in turned wood shaped like a basset-horn, with gilt bronze ferrules at either end on which escutcheons are engraved. The baton carried by the Great Elector of Brandenburg, encased in blue velvet, richly embroidered in gold and silver thread, was used in the solemnities at that prince's interment in 1688, and afterwards became part of the crown jewels of Prussia.

During the nineteenth century the marshal's baton came to be thought of less as an object for use on the field than as a symbol of the authority and honour vested in its possessor. The Emperor William II of Germany issued a mandate prescribing the occasions on which the sovereign should carry the marshal's baton—regulations which could, of course, only apply to himself, and yet only a few weeks after the promulgation of this important decree he appeared at the unveiling of the Bismarck memorial in Berlin with a riding-whip in his hand!

With the emergence and organisation of a standing army in Prussia officers and non-commissioned officers took to carrying the cane, or spontoon, and were not slow to employ it in merciless chastisement of unfortunates whose evil star had led them to enlist. This was not peculiar to Prussia. "All over Austria the 'almighty stick' provides a ready answer to all questions," writes Riesbeck in the letters on his Austrian travels published in 1780. It was an age in which both military and civil authority ruled by the rod; and when students lit their famous bonfire on the Wartburg they burned a Prussian military corset, a Hessian soldier's pigtail and an Austrian corporal's cane as three emblems of a time and a régime which was to be done away with for ever.

In the sixteenth century there was a prevailing fear of poison and of treacherous wiles of all sorts. Princes, who were most exposed to such dangers, were the first to consider means of protection, and took to sword-sticks, that is to say harmless-looking walking-sticks in which rapiers were concealed. The lector of Saxony had made for him by a resden armourer (either Hans Fleischer or Hans Frost) a long sword-stick consisting of n etched rapier-blade and a bone stick. On is death in 1596, Archduke Ferdinand of yrol left a walking-stick: "a Spanish blade ithin it and a dagger concealed in the gilt andle." This invention is not yet obsolete. word-sticks are still sought after, and the emand will probably increase in countries here the hooligan and "red" elements are ncouraged rather than suppressed by the w. The Berlin Police Museum contains a mall, apparently very harmless, walking-tick, which closer investigation reveals to be most cunningly constructed weapon, cap-ble of being bared for combat forthwith by nscrewing the handle; it was taken from a

KNOB OF
WALKING-STICK
"BEC DE CORBIN"

riminal who had murdered a government official with it. 'hus the stick may not merely *serve* as a weapon, but may ctually be specially adapted as a weapon.

Hollow sticks for smuggling, or other purposes which an ill bear the light of day, are of course, no modern nvention. The first cocoons of the silkworm to enter Europe (their export from China being punishable with death) vere carried across the frontiers at the peril of their lives by oilgrims using hollow staffs and were thus brought to Byzantium. The ingenious René, titular monarch of Sicily, vho died in 1480, possessed in his castle of Angers a walking-tick hollowed out to contain a portrait of his second wife, Jeanne de Laval, painted on a roll of parchment.

Walking-sticks as used now were unknown to the early Middle Ages. Old men leaned on sticks, the crooked stick or crutch being mentioned in the *Erec* in this connection, and oot-travellers carried them on their wanderings, but the walking-stick as a toy of fashion does not appear till the ifteenth century. Charlemagne had a stick described by the

Monk of St. Gall, but this was no doubt carried by him as sign of authority and not as a mere elegant superfluity whic he could just as well have done without.

The walking-stick of fashion is first heard of towards th close of the fourteenth century. An inventory in 1379 the goods of Charles V of France mentions cedar-wood stick with golden knobs, one bearing the arms of France, the othe those of the dauphin. A century later King René possesse a number of sticks (besides that mentioned above containin his wife's portrait); one was black, carved from end to en and covered with sweet-smelling lac, one white, with an ambe rosary attached to the handle, one adorned with peacock feathers, and so on; each had a sharp iron ferrule at the lowe end, like an alpenstock. Ivan the Terrible, when in friendl conversation with a subject, had a playful way of driving th iron spike of his stick through his foot, thus literally nailin him to the spot. Woe to the unfortunate who showe irritation at this little habit of the Czar!

When the stick became an article of fashion the ladie also adopted it. It is true that, at an earlier period, w learn that certain women of rank held sticks in their hands but these seem to have been rare exceptions. At the Syno of Orleans the Queen, wife of the Capet King Robert II, knocke out her confessor's eye with one, believing she detected heres in him. In the fifteenth century ladies were perhaps les violent in repartee; they merely imitated the gentlemen, a Martial d'Auvergne tells us, by carrying small walking-stick in their hands.

From this time on the walking-stick was regularly used b men, though it appears at first to have been adopted onl by the upper classes. In England Henry VIII, the roya Bluebeard, seems to have been the first to adopt the walking stick. His wardrobe in Greenwich Palace contained a numbe of walking-sticks, among them six covered in silk and orna mented with gold, one adorned with silver gilt and furnishe with an astronomical watch in the knob, and one whicl had a veritable tool-chest in its handle, for it was ornamente gold and had at the upper end a perfume-flask, beneath is a sundial and furthermore a pair of pincers, a compass, a ard-measure, a knife, a file, all in gold, and a golden touch-one. In the Dresden Historical Museum there is an Italian alking-stick with a silver knob of exquisite craftsmanship, earing the date 1540. Duke Albert of Bavaria used a stick ade of four pieces of ivory held together by means of nine old rings, the rings being set with sixty-four antique cut ones, small diamonds and rosettes in gold-enamel; the head as a circular sundial in gold; this remarkable piece of work, hich Philip Hainhofer admired in the art gallery of the Iunich Embassy in 1611, is now in the Wittelsbach Treasury. he Emperor Maximilian II, on his death in 1578, left the rchduke Wenceslas "a stick belonging to the Emperor erdinand with the royal Austrian arms" which was valued t forty florins.

In France Henry IV seems to have owned the first stick hich could be classed as an article of luxury. Under the ist of the Valois walking-sticks were not in use and Louis XIII sed a plain ebony stick with an ivory handle, but it was in is time that richly ornamented walking-sticks began to be ought after. An inventory of the Imperial Treasury in Vienna aken in 1619 describes some very costly specimens. One was f Indian wood with an amber handle, but this was the most nodest of the collection. Another, of Brazilian wood, had handle of oriental jasper mounted in gold and tipped with ilver; a third was of ebony, plated with gold and set with ubies and turquoises; a fourth was inlaid with mother-of-earl and set with eight rubies and seventeen turquoises; a ifth was of bamboo with gold plating in which were set nineteen arge turquoises and eighteen rubies. The gem of the collection, nowever, was a staff of Indian whalebone, plated with gold t the top, in which was a ring set with a fine diamond and a ine ruby, a cornelian, a sapphire, an emerald, an opal, an methyst, a topaz, and a chrysolite.

After examining this inventory one can no longer fairly harge Louis XIV with having first introduced excessive

luxury in the matter of walking-sticks. None the less he i
reputed to have been very fond of beautiful sticks, and h
broke across a lackey's back in a fit of temper a specimen mad
of rosewood. In 1695 the court jeweller procured for him
stick with an eagle knob set with twenty-four diamonds. Th
king never showed himself in public without a cane, a usag
which was immediately imitated by the other potentates
great and small. The fashion plates issued by the firm o
Bonnard in the second half of the seventeenth century an
often representing the "Grand Monarch" always show hin
cane in hand. It was a different matter for subjects. I
the days of Louis XIV no one, except the chief finance ministei
had the right to appear before the king with a walking-stick
The Emperor Leopold I had a stick set with turquoises an
diamonds. King Frederick III of Denmark, who made gol
in his leisure hours, had one with a handle of alchemistic gold
reputed to be of his own making. At the Rosenborg ma
also be seen other sticks which belonged to this first monarcl
of the Danish dynasty, among them some of narwhal-tusk
the handles and ferrules enamelled and set with rubies, anc
a "Jacob's staff and rhyme stick" in silver, dated 1663. Hi
son the future King Christian V, who died in 1699, when Crowi
Prince carried a silver-plated walking-stick with a yard measur
attached and various other instruments, such as a calibr
gauge, a compass and a sundial.

King Frederick I of Prussia, while still Electoral Prince
was presented by the Abbot of Murbach with a stick the handl
of which was of agate set with thirteen diamonds. Thi
monarch, as is well known, was extraordinarily fond of splendour. His successor, Frederick William I, took bediamondec
walking-sticks, one might almost say by the dozen, from hi
father's treasury—in 1713 one with five big and twenty-three
small brilliants; another with a head of coco-nut-wood, crownec
with a brilliant and eight rose-cut stones; another whose jaspe
handle was adorned with rubies and rose-cut stones; and ir
1719 ten more similar walking-sticks. Frederick I loved tc
receive such sticks as presents, and his third wife, Sophia Louisa

108

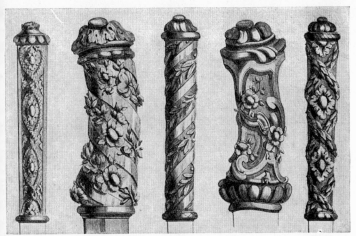

Designs by Maria   WALKING-STICK KNOBS   *Paris, c. 1760*

f Mecklenburg, gave him a stick with a gold knob in which
vas set a large table-cut stone backed in red.

Seventeenth-century sticks were very long and were usually
rasped below the actual handle. The handle itself was
ordinarily a round knob, often carved in relief. In the Court
Museum, Vienna, is a walking-stick knob cast in silver, of French
vorkmanship, showing Hercules in combat with Antæus.
Holes were bored through sticks near the upper end for the
purpose of threading through straps whose ends were secured
by tassels. Fashionable ladies of that time had already begun
o use similar sticks.

The eighteenth century was almost as much the age of the
tick or cane, as of the fan; no hand was without one and a
high degree of artistry and effort were expended on beauti-
ying the handle. The staff itself was usually of Bengal cane,
out for the handle practically all workable materials were
used. Very occasionally other materials besides Bengal cane
or wood were chosen for the staff. In the Court Museum,
Vienna there is a small walking-stick made of tortoiseshell
with the crowned double-headed eagle design on its golden
knob handle. In the Green Vault in Dresden are walking-

sticks of Cingalese serpent-wood and of so-called unicorn horn which is really moulded tortoiseshell. A walking-stick which belonged to the Archduke Charles Augustus of Zweibrücken who died in 1795, was made of tortoiseshell with a gold enamelled knob, but these are exceptions, probably for the good reason that such cast or moulded specimens had to be treated very tenderly to avoid breaking; to employ them as cudgels, as the mighty ones of those days were very fond of doing, would have been calamitous. Frederick William I of Prussia is an example of this type of ruler; in his fits of fury he did not spare his own family and chose men of middle-class origin as his ministers because they would put up with his beatings.

If the choice of suitable materials for the stick itself was somewhat restricted, there were no such limitations in regard to the handle. Here the restrictions were those of form. Only three basic shapes were employed; the round knob (which might be polygonal) commonly used in the seventeenth century; the crook, which could really be used to lean upon; and the slightly curved handle which the French call "bec de corbin." These three forms of handle were carried out in precious stones, semi-precious stones, gold, silver, bronze, ivory, mother-of-pearl, amber or horn, and the china industries of Meissen, Vienna, Berlin and Chantilly were no sooner in being than they took zealously to the making of heads of walking-sticks, endowing them with all the charm of the trivial yet dainty rococo style of art. King Charles III's porcelain factory in Naples supplied eighteen different models of walking-stick handles, at from one to sixty ducats the piece.

There was room for extravagant expenditure in the matter of walking-sticks, and in France bankers and farmers of taxes spent more recklessly than any. Samuel Bernard, who went bankrupt so often that his wealth eventually grew beyond his computation, and de la Popelinière are said to have possessed walking-sticks worth about ten thousand talers. People of fashion spent as much as forty thousand francs a year on walking-sticks. The Duc de Richelieu, famed as a lady-killer (more famous, indeed, in this field than as an army commander)

Designs by Lalonde   *Paris, c. 1780*

WALKING-STICK KNOBS

lso distinguished himself by the taste and costliness of his
valking-sticks. Even Voltaire, who of course despised fashion,
ossessed eighty walking-sticks, and Rousseau, who was a
oor man, had forty. In Germany the Prime Minister of
axony, Count Brühl, probably owned more numerous and
andsomer specimens than anyone else. He was the fortunate
ossessor of three hundred canes, one for each of his three
undred suits, and with each a snuff-box to match!

Such a vast demand naturally taxed the inventive powers
f the makers of walking-stick handles to the utmost. The
lector of Saxony possessed a walking-stick with a knob cut
ut of an emerald. The Elector Maximilian Joseph III of
3avaria had a cane with a knob made of an amethyst set in
hirty brilliants and another of green jasper encased in gold
iligree, containing, under glass, a tiny watch by C. Cabrier
f London. The same monarch also possessed a cane with a

III

handle in the form of a lion's head, set with five hundred
and forty-eight brilliants and three hundred and twenty-two
emeralds. In the Ole Olsen collection there is a walking-stick
handle in grey cornelian, carved like a Turk's head, the eyes
in enamel, with surrounding garlands triply carved in gold
and silver. An inventory taken in 1731 of the Viennese
Treasury mentions numerous walking-sticks set with rubies,
diamonds, emeralds, and garnets, among them one of Bengal
cane with a gold knob crowned with a large emerald in a ring
of small diamonds, and another with a gold knob adorned with
one big and eight small diamonds. There were also numerous
sticks which could be used as field-glasses, usually with watches
in their gold-filigree knobs.

The desire to make walking-sticks useful as well as ornamental led to their adaptation as telescopes and pedometers.
The Mathematical Salon in Dresden houses three pedometer
walking-sticks. The earlier two of the three are not dated, but
the latest is signed "Lehmann Reinharz" and accordingly
must have come from the workshop of Löser, Count of
the Holy Roman Empire, about the year 1740. At the close
of the walking-stick-loving century the "czakan," or walking-
stick-flute was invented, a long flute in walking-stick form
which became very popular in Austria and Hungary. In
respect of usefulness a walking-stick placed in the Viennese
Treasury in 1750 probably holds the palm. It was "a long
stick in three sections which could be unscrewed. In the lowest
was a writing quill with all necessary accessories, in the next
a measuring-rod, and in the third a telescope. The hollow
knob is intended to contain a sweet-scented sponge." For
dancing-masters, who needed to accompany their pupils on
the fiddle, and used very small instruments which they could
carry in the pocket for this purpose, there were walking-sticks
which could be converted into fiddles. The Cluny Museum in
Paris exhibits such a "canne-pochette" made of tortoiseshell
inlaid with silver, the stick being of ebony.

King Frederick the Great of Prussia, who spent less on his
whole household in a year than other courts often squandered

PLATE V

COLONEL OF THE FRENCH ARTOIS DRAGOONS

After Le Clerc.   From the "Galerie des Modes."   1778

n a single festivity, nevertheless made a special hobby of nuff-boxes and walking-sticks; where these were concerned e was less penurious than usual. The merchant Gotzkowski upplied him with a crook for a walking-stick made of mother-f-pearl mounted in gold at a cost of 125 talers; Messrs. Jordan, ourt jewellers, with a gold walking-stick knob for 35 talers, jasper "bec de corbin" mounted in gold and set with diamonds or 360 talers, a round knob in enamel with brilliants for 2,270 alers, a crook in various sorts of gold for 1,400 talers, a knob of ock crystal mounted in gold and richly set with brilliants for ,500 talers, the stick itself being reckoned at 16 talers.

After Frederick's death three walking-sticks were found at anssouci, one with a crook-handle of chrysoprase, set with rilliants one with a crook of gold and one with a steel crook ilded to look like gold. In the palace at Potsdam where rederick spent his winters was found a walking-stick with a old enamelled crook, which Napoleon carried off in 1806 and resented to Marshal Ney, whence by many devious routes it eturned at last to the possession of the Prussian royal family. The Hohenzollern Museum in the Palace of Monbijou contains et another crook-handled walking-stick of Frederick's, made f solid tortoiseshell, the handle, enclosing a telescope, being nlaid in gold and mother-of-pearl.

Arthur, Count zu Solms, had a walking-stick crook made out f stag's antlers; it comprised a hunting-watch mounted in the orn, the lower end of which, shaped like a hound with a ring n its mouth, formed a hunting whistle, while at the upper end he watch, its face protected by a case, was set in a strong ilver mount; on the outer side this showed a silver medallion hased with a representation of a christening and the name of he artist, "Bruberger," while on the reverse side was the nscription, "This remarkable stag was shot by me on the day f the baptism of my son Adolf, 1st October, 1750. Arthur, Count zu Solms."

Naturally enough walking-sticks were much used as presents n those days. In 1733 the Emperor Charles VI gave his elative, the heir-apparent of Brunswick-Bevern, a walking-

stick with a handle of lapis lazuli, set with a large brillia
besides smaller diamonds and rubies. In 1777 Catherine
presented King Gustavus of Sweden with a stick set wit
diamonds to the value of 60,000 roubles, about £10,000
pre-war money. Franklin received from the Countess Palatir
of Zweibrücken a walking-stick made from the wood of a wi
apple-tree with a gold knob in the shape of a "cap of Liberty
He gave it to his friend Washington, saying that if it were
sceptre it would be worthy of him and would be well wielde
in his hand. In the *corbeilles* of French princesses, containir
the valuables which it was customary that they should preser
to their suites, walking-sticks found a place, and in the *co*
beille of the Infanta of Spain, who married the Dauphin i
1745, were fifteen walking-sticks *à bec de corbin* costing i
all 3,600 francs, to be distributed to subaltern officers.

All through the eighteenth century the cane was as indi:
pensable to the man of the world as his sword, as necessar
to the lady of fashion as her fan. Corvinus, who wrote unde
the pen-name of "Amaranthes," mentions in 1715 "the walking
stick, a thin or flexible staff made of Bengal cane, with a loo
attached," and although in England in 1730 fashion dictate
that this "flexible staff" should be exchanged for a stout oa
stick, the mark of the true gentleman under Queen Anne an
George I was still the elegance with which he manipulated hi
cane or walking-stick. There is a story that Louis XV onc
threw his walking-stick out of a window in Versailles to avoi
the temptation of laying it about the shoulders of the Duc d
Lauzun, who at the moment was boring him to distraction.

In Paris, the very centre of elegance, a distinction was mad
between the "badine," or switch, and the walking-stick proper
and it was correct to carry them at different hours of the day
Sebastien Mercier, who has described Parisian life at differen
periods, writes in 1782: "In the forenoon the switch is carried
it makes walking more speedy and there is an end of the quarrel
and disputes so common sixty years ago, when bloodshed wa
deemed necessary to expiate some mere oversight. The ladie
go out and take exercise in the streets and on the boulevards

114

FASHION-PLATE
From the "Galerie des Modes"

walking-stick in hand. It is no mere toy for them; they need t more than the men, for their high heels increase their stature it the expense of their capacity to walk."

Since 1770 the Parisian physician Tronchin had been advising ladies to take plenty of exercise, and especially to go for walks, as a remedy for that fashionable ill, "the vapours." For this purpose, of course, they needed the walking-stick, and they made willing and industrious use of it as pictures show in the "Galerie des Modes" in Bertuch's *Journal des Luxus und der Moden*. They were supplied with pretty and attractive models in plenty. In the Bourgeois Collection, formerly at Cologne, there was a lady's walking-stick, 144 centimetres long, in red stained wood, ornamented in chased and gilded copper. The handle ended in a sharply curved "bec de corbin," and the

115

stick had an iron ferrule. Baron Rolas de Rosey's collection in Dresden contained a lady's walking-stick with an amber handle which opened with a double screw and could be used as a receptacle for two different perfumes. The lid disclosed an amorous picture beneath an amber mirror.

The constant and widespread use of the walking-stick gave rise to a code prescribing the manner of its display. De la Salle, who published a book of rules of deportment in 1782, gives a host of instructions for behaviour in this matter. The walking-stick might never be taken on visits to people of consequence. It was bad form to toy with it or to touch any other person with it, while to make as if to strike another was the worst of crimes against *bon ton*. The stick might not be held under the arm; it might not be leaned upon when standing, and to write in the dust with it when sitting was as improper as to trail it after one when walking.

The Republic did not abolish the stick but merely altered its form and its use. For example, it placed in the hands of the "Incroyables" no plaything, but a very solid cudgel with which to defend themselves against the ruffianly bands of Jacobins, driving those rowdies, who only attacked the un protected, to hunt in couples. How useful such walking-sticks would be against the hooligans of our own day! The "In croyables" (who were very stout fellows and by no means the mere clothes-props and fops which the party spite of those they had thrashed made them out to be) had a special means of recognising each other, a kind of Freemasonic secret greeting conveyed by a particular and agreed manner in which they handled their short thick sticks. Those years also, which were the hey-day of the rabble, saw the manufacture of vast numbers of sword- and dagger-sticks, for which all kinds of remarkable forms were invented.

The fashion for walking-sticks survived all phases of the Revolution, perhaps for the sole reason that men were glad to have *some* object to occupy idle hands, the ladies with their fans, muffs, pompadours or sunshades having so much the advantage of them in this respect. The Empire continued he use of different sticks for the forenoon and afternoon. ount Clary-Aldringen writes to his wife from Paris on 10 May, 810 that he is following the fashions himself "with a walking-tick in the mornings which must on no account be confused /ith the stick carried in the evening." Even Napoleon, who sually wore uniform, made some concessions to fashion and ossessed a tortoiseshell walking-stick with a musical box ttached.

The English gentleman was as inseparable from his cane s was his French counterpart. Some unknown author thought : necessary in 1809 to issue some very quaint rules of conduct or the carriers of walking-sticks to ensure as far as possible hat the grave risks to themselves and others should at least e restricted! He relates as a warning the cautionary tale of young man who loses the favour of his benefactress and herewith a great inheritance because he is so careless as o knock out the lady's two last remaining teeth with his ane, and she, unable to forgive this outrage, casts him off or ever!

Throughout the nineteenth century the walking-stick retained avour with gentlemen. It is only since every better-class man as felt it a duty to carry an attaché case about with him on ll occasions, even if it contains nothing but a newspaper and is luncheon sandwich, that the walking-stick has been forced omewhat into the background, for the simple reason that w men are deft enough to carry two objects at once without eing an intolerable nuisance to themselves and everyone else. ashion, naturally, has seen many changes in the size and hape of the handle and in Paris it was once *de règle* for the an of fashion to have his silver-crooked cane with him even the theatre.

Man and his walking-stick having become apparently nseparable, invention was exercised to make this article s attractive as possible. When, for example, La Harpe's vearisome tragedies were being produced in Paris, a knob-andled stick appeared which concealed a shrill whistle in the andle and which was named "the Barmecide stick" after

that dramatist's dreariest piece. During the Restoration a
reminders of the Empire were strongly repressed and th
careless were liable to bring punishment on themselve
Walking-sticks were then invented with oddly distorted knob
which, when held against a light, cast upon the wall the un
mistakable profile of the "petit caporal." In Germany studen
used their sticks as albums, getting their friends to writ
their names upon them until they were completely encircle
thus, from top to bottom. When, at the time of the persecu
tions of the demagogues, Arnold Ruge was cited before th
infamous Geheimrat von Kamptz, he carried such a stic
during the trial and aroused the suspicions of that persecuto
Long after the young student had gone his way, the Prussia
Geheimrat sent police in pursuit of him to deprive him of th
dangerous implement!

Inventors and merchants have competed to exploit th
technical possibilities of the walking-stick by the use eith
of the handle or the staff. One Hemmer invented a walkin
stick lightning-conductor; wires could be pulled out at eith
end, one to be planted in the earth while the other projecte
some eight or nine feet into the air, the idea being that if th
possessor then moved a certain distance from the stick he woul
be secure from lightning. In 1817, Horn of Dresden co
structed a walking-stick which could be transformed into
lantern. But that was not all. In 1894 a French newspap
reproduced twenty-two designs by means of which a walkin
stick could be adapted as a tripod for a camera, as a toile
table, as a painter's easel, as a footstool, as a chair, as a sho
gun, as a candle-stick and as a lantern. The handle containe
knife, fork and spoon, a hammer for mineralogy, a photographi
camera, pen and ink, a pistol, a drinking-glass, a tobacco-cas
surgical instruments, a box of matches, a cigarette case,
telescope, a flint, etc. Since then there have appeared walkin
sticks containing family medicine - chests, walking-sticks t
be used as ear-trumpets, and a number of other cunning d
vices, and one only hopes that the happy possessors of suc
magnificent contrivances always have them at hand when th

moment of usefulness arrives and are not like the owners of umbrellas who have invariably left them at home when it comes on to rain!

The many forms of the walking-stick aroused the interest of the collector. Heine relates that Heinrich Beer of Berlin, brother of the composer Meyerbeer, had a collection of walking-sticks worth 6,000 talers. In 1880 at the auction of the contents of the Palace of San Donato near Florence, twenty-six valuable walking-sticks belonging to Prince Anatole Demidoff came under the hammer and fetched up to 1200 francs apiece.

WALKING-STICK
KNOB IN GOLD
AND ENAMEL

GREEK LADY WITH A PARASOL
From a vase painting in the Hamilton Collection

CHAPTER V

PARASOLS AND UMBRELLAS

OF those two near relations, the sunshade and the umbrella
the sunshade is the older, and that by some two thousand
years. It comes from the East, where the climate makes some
shelter from the sun's fierce rays imperative. It was and is
a useful, indeed an indispensable, adjunct of life in hot countries,
and it was because persons of high rank did not carry it themselves, but had it carried over them, that it became a symbol
of power and dignity. Alabaster reliefs in Nimrod's palace
at Nineveh, believed to date from between 885 and 860 B.C.
show the Assyrian ruler in his war chariot, and behind him
stands a slave with a parasol to shield him from the burning
rays of the sun; the parasol is conical, made of some striped
material, and, as far as can be judged, made to fold up. In

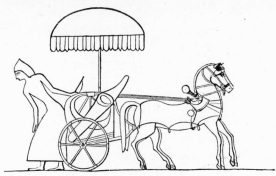

EGYPTIAN CHARIOT WITH PARASOL
After a wall painting in Thebes

the case also of the Achæmenidæ, who ruled in Persepolis, a parasol-bearer walks behind the royal car. In ancient Egyptian art the pharaohs are shown enthroned beneath the parasol, and images of gods carried in procession are protected by parasols. Pictures in ancient Thebes show princesses driving in small chariots to which fringed sunshades are attached. They were in general use in ancient Persia, for Xenophon writes in his *Cyropædia* that the Persians use sunshades in the hot season of the year. It is doubtful if they were known to the Hebrews of old, for there is no apparent reference to them in the Bible; if they were adopted it must have been late in Jewish history and probably they were derived from Greece. The earliest known representation of one is upon a coin of the time of Herod Agrippa, who died in A.D. 44; the parasol shown on this coin has a fringe.

How long a history lies behind the parasol in the Far East cannot be ascertained, but that it existed in China in the eleventh century B.C. can be proved. There it has long been an emblem of rank. While the mandarins ruled in the Middle Empire, the rank of any holder of office could be judged according to whether a double- or triple-decked umbrella was carried over him; a *fourfold* sunshade was the privilege of the heaven-born Emperor alone. Accounts of early missionaries in China portray in lively colours the procession of the Emperor to the Great Pagoda. Two hundred gilt and be-dragoned fans and twenty-four magnificent parasols were carried in procession and, before the Emperor himself, a particularly resplendent sunshade in silk and gold, adorned with flowers, feathers and precious stones. When in 1897 the German ambassador went from Peking to Wuchang he was given a ceremonial reception there by the Chinese authorities. "They actually had waiting for him a red silk umbrella, the sign of executive authority!" writes his wife in a letter. In May 1898 Prince Henry of Prussia visited the Emperor of China and the great ruler received him under a red umbrella. In Japan also the parasol has its place in all outdoor processions and ceremonies and the Mikado never appears in public unaccompanied by his parasol-bearer.

The sunshade may be of equal antiquity in India. Reliefs on the right-hand pillar of the east tower of the great stupa of Bhilsa, the earliest examples of Indian art under Persian influence and probably dating from about the time of the birth of Christ, show an assembly of gods enthroned, over whose heads female slaves carry parasols.

Kalidasa mentions the sunshade in his *Sakuntala*. In his fifth incarnation Vishnu descends into the underworld with processions of Brahmins accompanying his chariot with parasols made of costly materials, set with pearls and precious stones. In India also the sunshade was a sign of rank and a parasol with seven coverings was the emblem of the monarch. In an address by the King of Burma to the Governor-General of India in 1855 the monarch calls himself "Lord of the Great Parasol" and the Mahratta princes have never ceased to bear this title. When in 1877 the then Prince of Wales made a tour of India he rode upon an elephant and had a golden parasol carried above him to inspire the respect of the Indian populace. He brought home with him a large collection of magnificent umbrellas, the gifts of Indian princes, some entirely covered with feathers, some embroidered. The costliest of all came from the Begum of Oude and was of blue silk, stitched in gold thread and covered all over with real pearls. The sunshade was for long practically unknown in Europe and it struck

LADY WITH PARASOL-BEARER
From a Grecian vase in the Berlin Museum

early travellers in India as a notable feature of that country. "No one who thinks himself a person of any consequence in Goa appears on foot in the street, but has himself carried by slaves in a palanquin with a great "quitesol," or sunshade, to protect him from the heat of the sun and also for pomp and show," writes Mandelsloh in his account of his eastern travels, published in 1633. Sunshades in ordinary use in China and Japan are made with a bamboo frame and a cover of oiled paper, gaily printed with coloured pictures and mottos.

In classical Greece the parasol was used to protect the sacred offerings as they were carried in procession to the temples of Athene, Ceres, Poseidon and other divinities, and also at the feasts of Dionysus. But it had secular uses also. Anacreon makes merry over one Artamon who used a parasol with an ivory handle, just like a woman's. Their construction must have been very like the modern, for they were made to fold up.   In Aristophanes's *Knights*, Agoracritus says to Demos "Thine ears were spread out like a parasol, and then furled again," while in the same poet's *Thesmophoriazusæ* the Chorus of Women boast that they have not thrown away their parasol as the men have their shields.   Greek vase paintings show the parasol as an article of familiar use; women sit with it, or walk accompanied by slaves holding it over them.   In solemn processions not slaves but daughters of the μέτοικοι, or alien settlers, bear the parasols.   On the engraved metal mirrors also which have been found in such numbers in Etruscan tombs, the sunshade is shown as a common article of female use.   The shape seems to have been inspired by certain pointed head dresses worn by the women of Greece, and possibly still in vogue, in parts of Japan, Korea, and China.   The handle was not always in the middle but was often attached at the edge, an arrangement which must have been particularly convenient when the owner had it carried behind her by a slave as she walked, for it enabled her to get the full benefit of the shade it cast.

The sunshade used by the ladies of Rome probably differed in no way from that used in Greece.   According to Pliny, palm leaves were used to make the cover and bamboo canes for the frame.   Later the cover was made of silk, dyed in purple and ornamented with gold, while the frame and handle were of ivory set with gems.   Pollux, Ovid and Martial mention the sunshade and the Roman custom of having it held over the owner by a slave.   In ancient Rome, moreover, the umbrella as a protection not against sun, but against rain, appears to have originated; at least, there are various passages in the Latin classics which can hardly be interpreted otherwise. Virgil, in the second book of the Georgics, speaks of an umbrella made of leather, which can hardly have been a sunshade, and Martial, in an epigram in his fourteenth book, says: "Do not forget, when you go out in fair weather, to take an umbrella in case of bad weather."   Juvenal cannot mean a sunshade when he recommends a "beautiful green umbrella . . . because the wet spring season draws nigh."   Originally, no doubt, the

Calcutta, 1848

CHATTA BURDAR. INDIAN BEARER WITH A STATE PARASOL

mbrella was part of the lady's toilet but, just as in Greece,
he men also must have found it far too useful not .to
se it.   In A.D. 399 Claudian mentions the umbrellas
whether for sun or rain is not made clear) which effeminate
oung men carry when walking, but later this custom must
ave become usual, for in a treatise on education attributed
perhaps mistakenly) to Boethius, we are told of the death of
he young son of a prætor from a sunstroke contracted for
vant of the precaution of carrying a sunshade in the dog days.
    Like fans and gloves, parasols were adopted as ritual orna-
nents by the Church, and thus saved to survive in medieval

culture. The clergy adopted them less as objects of practica
use than in their typically Eastern aspect as symbols of powe
and dignity. As with many another privilege, the Pope claime
not only the right to use the umbrella himself but also to bestov
it on other persons as an emblem of authority. Pope Paul
(757–767) presented Pippin the Short with an umbrella
Miniatures of the Carlovingian period—for example one in
psalter in the library at Utrecht—show King David shelteree
by an angel with an umbrella, which if the artist has bee
faithful to his model, would appear to have been made with
collapsible frame. An intaglio of Bishop John of Pavia (884
942) shows him followed by a servant with an outsprea
umbrella. It is probable that the "Schutzdach" (coverin
roof, in modern German literally "shed") sent by Bisho
Alcuin of Tours about 800 to Bishop Arno of Salzbur
"to protect your venerable head from showers" was a tru
umbrella (nowhere more useful than in Salzburg), or may i
not possibly have been a very large hat?

In ceremonies at the papal court the umbrella filled th
double rôle of a useful article and a symbol. Whenever th
Pope appeared in public an open umbrella was carried ove
him. Ulrich von Reichental, a canon and the author of
detailed illustrated account of the proceedings at the Counc
of Constance from 1414 to 1418, has not omitted to portray th
entry of Pope John XXIII with pen and brush. A knigh
carrying a truly gigantic umbrella has not been forgotter
"Now it is well known," writes our reporter "that such
shelter is carried before a Pope when he wishes to ride abroac
and is carried by a fully-armed man upon a white charge
with a red cloth adorned with gold, and is red and yellow an
is carried both for rain or sun so that he can enter in beneat
it. And above, upon the shelter, is a golden angel, and ha
a golden cross in his hand and the shelter was forty foot wide.
Red and yellow are the papal colours, being also those of th
city of Rome.

On the occasion of solemn processions and particularl
important ceremonies the Pope appeared accompanied by tw

126

KNIGHT WITH THE PAPAL UMBRELLA AT THE ENTRY
OF JOHN XXIII INTO CONSTANTINOPLE
Illumination in Ulrich von Reichenthal's MS.
"Concilium Constantiense"

umbrella-carriers, one bearing an open and one a closed umbrella
symbolic of the spiritual and temporal powers. The umbrellas
themselves preserved their traditional oriental form and might
have served twelve centuries earlier at the court of the Achæ-
nenidæ. The papal court is the only one which retains the
umbrella as an emblem of power and dignity to this day.
Apart from this it has taken refuge in heraldry, where in conical
form and accompanied by the two keys it represents the
papacy. As long as the Ecclesiastical States remained independent this symbol had a place in their escutcheon. In the
great Roman basilicas the umbrella still hangs, in the papal
colours, and is used in processions to this day. This large

127

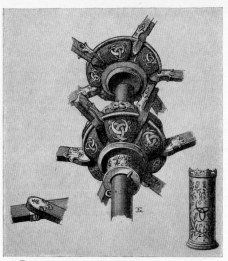

DETAILS OF THE FRAME OF AN UMBRELLA
Once the property of Diane de Poitiers. Reiset Collection

form of umbrella was the model for that smaller one with which
the Catholic Church protects the Sacrament of the Altar when
it is carried through the streets to the sick and dying.

Like the Pope, the Doge of Venice used the umbrella as an
emblem of dignity. The custom of protecting the Doge's
head with an umbrella of cloth of gold whenever he appeared
in public with his full suite can be traced back to 1176 and
persisted till the Republic came to an end. Goethe in his day
saw the ceremony performed. Since the mid-thirteenth
century, however, when the feast of Corpus Christi began to
be celebrated—thanks to the sunny season at which it occurs
—with yearly increasing pomp and splendour the baldachino,
supported on poles, has almost entirely ousted the umbrella
from religious processions, leaving it solely to Rome and to
the Head of the Church.

In the Middle Ages the laity saw the umbrella in church,
but, so far as can be discerned, nowhere else, for it seems to
have served no profane uses at that time. Tradition is silent,
or is content to give us hints from which little can be gathered.

PLATE VI

LADY WITH WALKING-STICK-SUNSHADE

*From Bertuch's " Journal des Luxus und der
Moden."* June 1791

Van Dyck

HELENA GRIMALDI, WIFE OF NICOLO CATANEO
P. A. B. Widener Collection

UPPER PORTION OF A POSTER   1715
"Parapluyes et parasoles à porter dans la poche"

The Normans are said to have possessed a form of umbrell,
consisting of twelve or more separate parts, though it is doubtfu
if it could be folded up, and, coming as they themselves di
from a rainy climate, to have introduced it into England a
early as the eleventh century. However that may be, all trac
of it must have been lost, for if it fell into lay hands anywhere
this must surely have been in Italy. When the umbrella—
that is to say that form of it which we call the parasol—onc
more emerges from obscurity we find it in Italy, and n
earlier than the sixteenth century. *Dasypodius's Dictionarium*
published in Strasbourg in 1537, recognises the word "Sonnen
schirm" (or sunshade) as current, but the parasol certainly wa
not in general use at that period, since there is a total absenc
of reference to it in contemporary art and literature. Th
earliest relic we have of it—and that but a fragment—is
portion of the frame of a parasol which belonged to Diane d
Poitiers, who, as mistress of Henry II of France, was no doub
likely to be the first woman to possess any novel articles o
fashion and elegance introduced in her day.

The parasol cannot have been at all generally used in Ital
during the first half of the sixteenth century, as otherwis
Catherine de' Medici, who introduced so many customs of he
native land into France, would certainly have brought th
sunshade with her. Again no mention is found of it in a
inventory of those articles of luxury which Henry III and hi
minions considered to be the essentials of an elegant life
and this again is proof of rarity. It is not till the last third

of the century that we begin to meet references to it. In 1578 Henri Estienne writes in his *Dialogues*: "Speaking of ans (flags), have you ever seen a device which certain persons of rank in Spain and Italy carry, or have carried, less to protect themselves against flies than against the sun? It is supported

THE LADY UNDER THE PARASOL
After Lancret.   Engraved by Boilvin

upon a stick, and it is so constructed that it takes up little room when it is folded; but when it is needed it can be opened forthwith and spread out in a round that can well cover three or four persons." In his travels through Italy in 1580 Montaigne noticed that the ladies of Lucca frequently had a sunshade in their hands, but its advantages do not appear to have dawned upon the French philosopher. In the third book of his *Essays*

131

c. 1760

"UMBRELLAS!" PARIS STREET-HAWKER

he remarks that "sunshades, which have been used in Ital᾽
since the days of the ancient Romans, are rather a burden to th᾽
arm than a protection to the head." In the trousseau o᾽
Princess Anna Catherina Gonzaga, who married the Archduk᾽
Ferdinand in 1582, was a sunshade of the estimated value o᾽
four ducats. Veronese, in his "Finding of the Infant Moses,"
has portrayed a black slave holding a sunshade over the hea᾽
of the princess, and Crispin de Passe gives parasols a place i᾽
his pictures of modes and manners.

Travellers visiting Italy in those decades often brought bac᾽
as mementoes brightly coloured little pictures of modes an᾽
costumes in the peninsula. An album of such drawings datin᾽
from 1587 and now in the Lipperheid Museum of Costume᾽
shows a picture of a mounted cavalier shielding himself from
the sun by means of a red parasol, green-fringed, entitle᾽

TWO GENTLEMEN DRIVING UNDER AN UMBRELLA
From the "Skizzenbuch der Danziger Reise," Chodowiecki

Thus one rides in Italy in summer." By about 1600 sunshades seem no longer to have been rarities in Italy. The
English traveller, Coryate, who visited that country in 1608,
describes the umbrella as "a small baldachino made of leather
with contrivances for opening it out," upon a wooden frame,
and he tells us that it was chiefly used when riding and that it
was very dear. Maria de' Medici, the second wife of Henry IV,
probably brought specimens with her from Italy to France,
for we learn that the dauphin, the future Louis XIII,
when he walked in the gardens in 1697 was sheltered by a
page with a parasol. They were still far from common, for
those which found their way to the Imperial Court were not
used but deposited in the treasury, an inventory of which,
taken in 1619, conscientiously notes down "five Turkish and
German umbrellas, for use in the sun." Philip Hainhofer also
mentions an "umbrella" as a noteworthy item in the picture
gallery at Ambras.

The sunshade was not unknown to the English poet Michael
Drayton, nor to Ben Jonson, and the French comedian,
Tabarin, who enjoyed his maximum popularity under Louis
XIII and got his effects largely by wearing a hat of improbably
enormous dimensions and playing all sorts of absurd tricks
with it, humorously asserted that the invention of both

sunshade and umbrella were due to his hat. Charles Lebrun
painting of Séguier's entry into Rouen in 1639 shows two page
carrying an umbrella over his head, and Van Dyck's portra
of the patrician Genoese lady, Elena Grimaldi, also depicts
sunshade, but at this date ladies and gentlemen are neve

LADY WITH A WALKING-STICK-UMBRELLA

Bertuch's "Journal des Luxus und der Moden"
September 1790

shown carrying the umbrella themselves, an indication that i
was still too clumsy in construction for persons of consequenc
to handle it.

The earliest seventeenth - century French umbrellas prov
that the wooden frame had already been abandoned in favou
of one of whalebone, but since the cover was made of oiled clotl

134

it was still very heavy and clumsy.   John Evelyn, who made
the grand tour through France and Italy with observant eyes,
noted many curiosities of the culture of his day and mentions
Italian umbrellas made of metal and straw, mushroom- and
bell-shaped.   On reaching Marseilles in 1644 he bought him-

LADY WITH A WALKING-STICK-UMBRELLA
Bertuch's "Journal des Luxus und der Moden"
July 1787

self an umbrella against the heat of the sun, and he was ex-
ceedingly interested in the first Chinese paper umbrella which
he saw in Paris on 22 June, 1664.   In 1665 Edward Browne
bought a sunshade in Venice, but the very fact that these
diarists find such events worth writing down shows that the
umbrella, in both its uses, was still a rare phenomenon in daily

135

life. The fact, too, that ladies such as Mlle Scudéry and the Marquise de Sévigné, and authors such as Ménage and Tallemant des Réaux, who took particular note of fashions, luxury, comfort and the mode, say nothing about the umbrella, affords further testimony to its rarity. Again, this may not be altogether unconnected with the fact that people of consequence in those days seldom walked, but used carriages and consequently needed no further protection against either sun or rain; should they walk a little way in the park, a servant would follow with an umbrella. An inventory taken in 1637 of the moveable property of the French Crown mentions eleven sunshades in various colours, made of taffeta, and three umbrellas (against rain) of oiled cloth, trimmed underneath with gold and silver lace.

Unremitting effort was devoted to devising a lighter and consequently more convenient article, and by the end of the century some progress had been achieved. The Bonnard fashion plates show young women, with clear pretensions to elegance, who carry the sunshade themselves and are not apparently overburdened. The philosopher Locke, who was in France in 1675, writes: "Sunshades are small, very light articles, used by the ladies here to shield themselves from the sun, and their employment seems to me very convenient." They were still heavy and bulky according to modern standards, although they were provided with rings by which they might be carried, as it were, upside down. The hobbledehoy youth of the umbrella lasted a full century after its rediscovery.

It was not till the eighteenth century that industrial enterprise took up the umbrella with some vigour, with the result that by the close of that era umbrellas and sunshades, which at its beginning had been little more than curiosities, had come to be regarded as essential parts of the wardrobe of both sexes. The predominance of the middle class element in all cultural questions had also largely contributed to this result; fashion during the course of the eighteenth century had tended increasingly towards simplicity, substituting wool for silk, dark colours for bright ones, boots for shoes and slippers, short-

CALEDONIAN BEAUTY

ut hair for long locks and powder. Aristocratic society, which had so long set the *ton*, had been accustomed to drive, ut middle-class society, to which the intellectual leadership ad gradually passed, went on foot. The umbrella had been

LADY WITH POMPADOUR PARASOL
Bertuch's "Journal des Luxus und der Moden," 1798

a mere plaything and toy to people of rank, but it becam
a necessity for the active, the working and professional classe

As early as 1710 one Marius of Paris had invented a
umbrella with a jointed stick which could be folded togethe
at the joint, placed in a case and carried in the pocket. Th
invention seems not to have fulfilled the expectations base
upon it, for it vanished without leaving a trace behind. I
England the "umbrella" was more popular than the "sur
shade." In 1710, Swift, in No. 238 of the *Tatler*, make
mention of it, and incidentally betrays the fact that it wa
made of oiled cloth at that date. It was assigned exclusively t
the fair sex, and the fact that on 12 December, 1709, a certai

138

LADY WITH POMPADOUR PARASOL
Viennese Modes, 1840

oung man borrowed an umbrella from a serving wench in
Vill's coffee-house in London was considered so remarkable that
was reported in the press. But it was among the English
ublic, in particular, that the umbrella—or rather the sun-
hade—achieved about that time a certain fame through the
art it played in Defoe's *Robinson Crusoe,* one of the most

widely read books in the literature of the world. The author makes his hero construct an umbrella after a pattern he had observed in Brazil and makes him describe the endless pain he took before he achieved his object. For lack of other material on his island, he made it from skins of animals. After the appearance of this novel in 1719 the sunshade was for a time known in England simply as the "Robinson."

In Germany the only protection used against rain hitherto had been great shawls known as "Regenkappen," but the umbrella has a place in Rädlein's dictionary, which was published in Leipzig in 1711. Gottlob Wilhelm Corvinus, who published his *Frauenzimmer-Lexikon*, or *Females' Dictionary* in 1715 under the pseudonym of Amaranthes, says: "Parasol means really a covering roof of oiled cloth supported upon a small pole, which females carry over their heads to protect themselves from the heat of the sun. In this country, however females use it when it rains. It can be opened and shut. The French give it the correct appellation and call it 'parapluye.'" Leupold, who in 1726 issued directions for the construction of a barometer in the form of a weather-house, gives a little woman with an open umbrella as a signal of bad weather, and thus Nehring appears to have been right when in 1736 he says in his *Historical and Political Lexicon* that "In hot countries the umbrella is used against the heat of the sun but in France and Germany it is used by females against rain and is therefore called the 'Regenschirm' (rain-shade)."

In any case it is safe to say that the umbrella and sunshade both existed and were differentiated after the first third of the eighteenth century, for if writers only mention umbrellas the *Frankfurter Intelligenzblatt* of the year 1734 advertises "small umbrellas with fringes against the sun, and large yellow and brown ones for rainy weather." In the same little newspaper in 1753 a lady announces that she has lost her green taffeta parasol trimmed with gold lace. It is said that umbrellas did not appear in Nuremberg till 1755.

Umbrellas, we have been told, were first seen in Venice in 1739 and sunshades about 1760, but pictorial art tells a different

PLATE VIII

VIENESSE MODE

1822

ory. The Venetian painters knew
e umbrella much earlier and it may
seen in Tiepolo's frescoes in the
lla Valmarana which date from
idway in the seventeen-thirties.
France also took early to the use
the umbrella; its manufacture
came a home industry, and there
e Parisian posters extant from about
20 in which makers of umbrellas
d parasols advertise their wares.
he jealous guild spirit among the
orkers however, gave the new in-
stry to the glovers, who are first
entioned in this connection in
50. Umbrellas were sold in the
reets of Paris by hawkers and criers
d cost anything from fifteen to
enty-two francs in 1754.

1841
UMBRELLA-HAWKER IN PARIS

Fashion seems to have adopted the umbrella rather suddenly,
r in 1768 Caraccioli writes: "For some time now it has been
e custom never to go out without an umbrella and to submit
the inconvenience of carrying it under the arm every day for
x months in order to use it, at a generous computation,
ssibly six times. Those, however, who do not wish to be
ken as belonging to the vulgar herd prefer to risk a wetting
ther than be looked upon as pedestrians in the street, for an
nbrella is a sure sign that one possesses no carriage." Bachau-
ont mentions in his journal that in 1769 a trading company
Paris acquired the privilege of hiring out umbrellas to the
ssers-by on the Pont Neuf.
From the middle of the eighteenth century, anyhow, the
nbrella and sunshade never lost ground, and in so far as they
ere subject to fashion, it became merely a question of change
colour, etc., and not of whether they should or should not
used. In 1788, for example, umbrella covers were white,
1789 green, in 1791 red, in 1804 blue; in 1787 sunshades in

141

eight different colours were carried, and so on. In 1754 sunshad
made to open and shut were for sale at from fifteen to twer
francs at The Hague. Inventors came forward with vari
ideas, not all of which could be called happy ones; in 17
for instance, one Dubourg constructed a "lightning-umbrell
with a metal spike earthed by means of a wire to which a me
ball was attached. Franklin's invention of the lightning-c

Dörbeck   *c.* 1825
From "Altberliner Redensarten"

ductor was the talk of the moment, but whether any purchas
was found indiscreet enough to draw down the lightning up
himself by means of this cunning device is not known—histo
thereafter is silent upon the subject!

In England the umbrella, it would seem, had to be p
petually rediscovered; at intervals it appears to have fall
into total oblivion. It is heard of in the seventeenth centu
and early in the eighteenth, and yet to this day in Engla
Jonas Hanway, who died in 1786, has the reputation not inde
of having invented, but of having introduced, the umbrel

142

o England. At any rate, he is said to have been the only
glishman during the last thirty years of the eighteenth
tury who never went out without an umbrella. Tradition
s it that he came across the umbrella upon his travels in
e East and was so impressed with its usefulness that he set
t to convert his fellow-countrymen to his point of view,
t met with such crass obscurantism as to be for years a
ure of fun to street-urchins before he could induce the

M. von Schwind   1847
From "Fliegende Blätter"

blic to employ this practical device. A certain Colonel
'olfe, visiting Paris in 1752, saw many people carrying
nbrellas and was surprised that this custom was still unknown
his native land; and things had not changed much even
venty or thirty years later. In 1775 the English consul at
myrna took home a sunshade from Leghorn and was positive
at such an article was almost totally unknown outside
ondon. It was first seen in Glasgow when a certain Mr.
mieson brought one from Paris in 1782.
But once England had become convinced of the advantages
the umbrella it was much used. It is obviously regarded

FASHION STUDIES
From "Fliegende Blätter" (1856)

as an everyday object in Gillray's caricatures, which appeare
during the final decade of the eighteenth century; indee
it seems possible that two novelties in connection with
originated in England about this time. The first is a form
sunshade with a jointed stick, permitting the outspread cov
to be tilted sideways so as to convert it into a kind of far
This device is known to Gillray in 1795 and first appears i
Germany in the pages of Bertuch's *Journal des Luxus und d*
Moden in 1798. It went out of fashion, but reappeared i
1860. The second novelty was the walking-stick-umbrella
a form derived no doubt from the long walking-sticks wit
which ladies were wont to support tottering footsteps o
heels of immoderate height, but having the great disadvar
tage that the dusty end became the handle when the owne
wanted to open her umbrella. The walking-stick-umbrell
was also short-lived, but became fashionable again in th
'seventies. There were also Englishmen, of course, amon
the ranks of the inventors, and in 1805 appeared the Englis
patent "paratout," so prettily named the "en-tout-cas" b
the ladies, being too big for use as a sunshade and too sma
when it rained!

In the meantime the umbrella had taken a place amidst th
triumphs of technical science, for the invention of the ai

144

FASHION STUDIES
From " Fliegende Blätter" (1856) .

alloon was speedily followed by that of the parachute. Not
ll umbrellas, however, were suitable for this sort of service,
nd when the French General Beurnonville, attempting to
scape from the Austrian military prison at Olmütz, used his
pen umbrella to descend from the top of a high wall it proved
sufficient to support his weight and a broken leg stopped
is farther progress.

During the nineteenth century, when the manufacture of the
mbrella passed to the factories, every effort was directed to
aking it lighter. The sixty patents taken out in the umbrella
dustry in France alone between 1791 and 1843 all had this
nd in view. The uncovered frame, which had weighed ten
ounds in 1806, had been reduced to a pound and half by 1826.
he final goal was reached in 1852 when a poor London artisan
amed Samuel Fox hit upon the happy notion of replacing
he heavy and clumsy whalebone frame by one of steel spokes,
n idea which is said to have brought him a fortune of about
300,000. The cover also was improved by the selection of
uitable material. In 1829 Messrs. Odiot set up in Paris a
actory for the manufacture of umbrella silk. Oiled cloth went
ltogether out of use, and for cheaper sorts cotton was
mployed. Alpaca appeared after 1848 and, in the 'seventies,
gloria," a silk mixture.

L

In the course of the nineteenth century the umbrella ha
once again the honour, even in the West, of becoming th
symbol of a dynasty, if you will, of a whole epoch. Loui
Philippe, King of the French, flirted with the *bourgeoisie* eve
before his accession, and when he succeeded his cousin o
the throne he diligently rid himself of all things conducin
to royal dignity and in all he did and left undone comporte
himself like a middle-class merchant. For example, he neve
went out without an umbrella. He used to say that a golde
crown was too cold for winter wear and too hot for summe
that a sceptre was too blunt to be used as a weapon and to
short for a walking-stick, and that a round felt hat and a goo
umbrella were far more useful on all occasions. Far fron
bringing him popularity this attitude merely won him th
nickname of "le roi Pépin," while the caricaturists of the da
(and France produced some brilliant ones) made the umbrell
the symbol of "M. Prudhomme," the type of the avaricious
hard-hearted, hypocritical, philistine townsman, who stood, t
them, for the "July Kingdom." How they laughed over th
National Guardsman who was inseparable from his umbrella
even when on sentry-go! But there was something in the spiri
of the age which favoured the umbrella, for the Duke of Welling
ton himself was never to be seen without one, and the hug

146

Caricature by Cham   1867

"Pardon! je ne savais pas que c'était la mode. J'ai cru que
vous aviez volé l'ombrelle de cette dame"

heavy cotton umbrella carried by King Frederick III of Denmark is preserved to this day as a relic in the museum at
the Rosenborg in Copenhagen.

Actually, the umbrella as a solemn symbol is a thing of the
past, though it crops up in occasional atavistic instances, as
when a lackey carried the dead woman's sunshade behind her
coffin at the funeral of the Princess Borghese, a daughter of
the Earl Talbot, in Rome in 1840, and when the last Khedive
but one confirmed the Coptic patriarch in his office by the
solemn presentation of an umbrella. In folk dress and customs,
however, it retained a certain symbolic value for a long time,
and in many parts of Germany till the end of last century a
red umbrella was invariably carried by the person appointed
to go round the neighbourhood with invitations to a wedding.

The sunshade was for long a purely feminine adjunct and
it was a concession to the Oriental point of view when
Queen Victoria presented the Sultan with one worth £3,000.

147

THE NEW ENGLISH UMBRELLA (1881)

It caused a considerable sensation when Spanish troops entered Hamburg in 1807 and the officers were seen to carry sunshades. Towards the end of the Second Empire, however, gentlemen began to carry sunshades of the same size as umbrellas, but whitish in shade and lined with some colour, such as dark blue. Fashion regarded the gentleman's umbrella as a matter of little consequence, it sufficed that it should be "quiet," though according to Gottfried von Böhm, the unhappy King Louis II of Bavaria seems to have regarded as one of his royal prerogatives the possession of the largest umbrella in the land. On one occasion he visited the Empress Elizabeth at Possen-hofen, wearing the uniform of a general and carrying in one hand his helmet and in the other his giant umbrella. The Empress happened to be standing at a window as he arrived and broke into a peal of laughter at his appearance—laughter which unfortunately proved infectious to some of His Majesty's own attendants. The King was furious. "Why should I risk spoiling my frisure?" he said angrily.

148

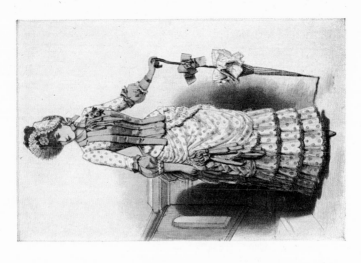

Plate IX

"LA MODE ARTISTIQUE," 1882

In ladies' fashions the sunshade, like all other matters connected with the mode, has seen many changes. At the beginning
of the nineteenth century it was very small. Goethe bought
four tiny sunshades for Christiane Vulpius at Carlsbad in May,
1800, at a cost of two talers, fourteen groats. The sunshade
might be more or less ornamental, with or without lace and
fringes, light or dark in colour, lined or unlined. In 1881
the first flame-coloured sunshades appeared, and were acclaimed
with jubilation in accordance with the then impressionistic
modes. After 1900 the sunshade began to grow rarer, a com-

From " Fliegende Blätter" (1901)

plexion of lilies and roses being less highly prized than formerly;
indeed, to be burnt coffee-brown had suddenly become the
dernier cri. This summer (1928) it has begun shyly—very
shyly—to creep back. Who knows if it may yet regain its
lost dominion?

The history of the umbrella as it appears in the comic
papers is a subject that really requires a chapter to itself.
In those happy days before public life was infected in every
part by the virus of politics and the *Münchener Fliegende
Blätter* could still publish harmless and amusing drawings free
of obscenity and be sure of a public to appreciate them, the

umbrella occupied a place of honour in the artist's repertoire,
side by side with the hat, the mother-in-law, the lieutenant,
and all the other time-honoured properties of the professional
jester. What countless numbers of times must Faust's speech
to Margaret—"Fair damsel, may I venture to offer you my
arm and escort?"—have been given a new interpretation by
the offer of an umbrella in a sudden shower of rain!
Tempi passati!

*Tournure-Parapluie, from
"Fliegende Blätter"* (1886)

CHAPTER VI

ORNAMENTS

Human culture begins with personal ornament, for it was not till man began to deck his body that he became conscious of his difference from the beasts. It is, indeed, impossible to over-estimate the influence of ornament in the evolution of man towards civilisation, for it was the origin of art and clothing, and was the basis of a psychological factor which created a thousand different associations and gave life fuller interest and value for the individual. Many races of men have come and gone of whose manner of life we should know nothing save for the trinkets and ornaments they left in their burial grounds.

The first and most urgent of life's problems is, of course, the provision of food, and it was probably to supply this need that man began to use weapons, grasping any stick or stone

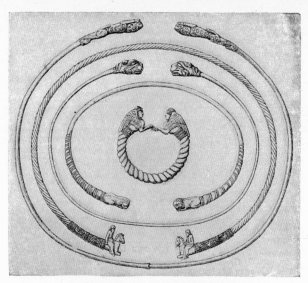

GREEK JEWELRY IN GOLD, FOUND IN THE CRIMEA
The Hermitage, St. Petersburg

that came to hand; but when hunger was satisfied, the desire for ornament must have asserted itself, and, indeed, the two impulses were closely linked, for the first ornaments displayed were claws and tusks taken by the primitive hunter from his prey to hang about his own body. Decorations of this kind can be traced back to the very earliest stages of human culture, and the only type of prehistoric man who does not appear to have used ornament is Neanderthal man, whom we believe to have lived a semi - animal existence. The forward step taken when man first began to adorn his body is important because he thereby marked himself off for ever from his origins; till then a beast among beasts, he suddenly became awake to his own personality. As Max Dessoir very truly says, "To adorn oneself is to emphasise one's individuality."

The evolutionary advance to ornament aroused man's vanity and opened up vistas not yet fully explored. Ornament of the body waked the first æsthetic impulses in the race; it

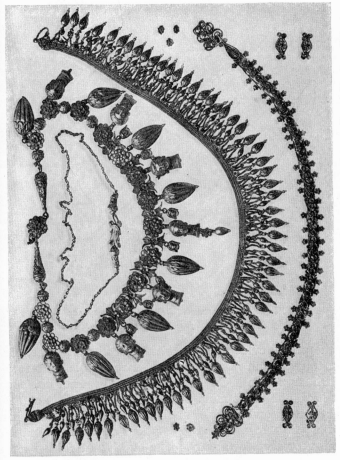

GREEK JEWELRY IN GOLD. OF THE BEST PERIOD, THE FOURTH TO THIRD CENTURY B.C.

153

Above: GOLD EARRING. *Below:* GOLD NECKLACE
Both of Greek Origin and found in a Grave in South Russia

was the primal evidence of a striving for higher values, of a
effort to realise an ideal. The first man who set out to dis
tinguish his person in some such way from that of his fellow
must have had in his mind the thought of the effect on *them*
that is to say, in whatever form his undertaking expressed itsel
it sprang from regard for the emotions of others. And her
lie the very roots of all art. The efforts put forth by tha
first man as he tried to render his appearance more strikin,
than that of his fellows, at the same time required the perceptio
of others to complete his purpose. No public, no artist. Th
first object of self-adornment must have been to impress other

154

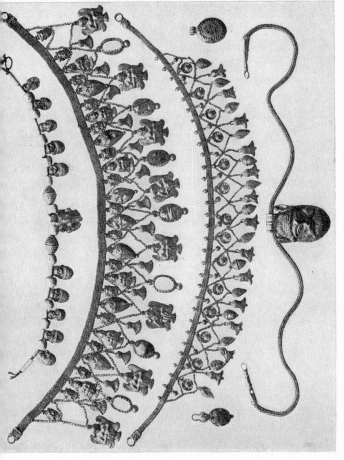

EARLY ETRUSCAN ORNAMENTS IN GOLD

Seventh to Sixth Century B.C.

—to please women, to instil awe among men, and to astonish both sexes. In attaining this end man discovered a visual language as universally understood as facial expression.

Emil Selenka, in his very able book, points out that the earliest form of ornament was designed simply to enhance and to emphasise the good points of the wearer. It thus possessed marked educational value, for it heightened the wearer's self-respect, set up a standard, encouraged him to

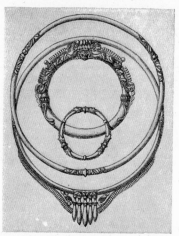

ETRUSCAN ORNAMENTS IN GOLD FOUND
IN THE RHINELAND

regulate his behaviour by the expectations his ornaments excited in others—in a word, *suggested* to him dignity, courage, enterprise, and so forth.

For our present purpose we may ignore the most primitive known forms of ornament, such as dressing of the hair by curling and frizzing and of the skin by scarring or tattooing, modes possible to man while he still went upon all fours. It was not till he stood upright that he could consider hanging ornaments upon his person, and his æsthetic sense must have developed to the point of distinguishing between "beauty" and "ugliness" before it occurred to him to collect odds and ends from in-

PLATE X

GIRL FROM MIESBACH. 1875

ETRUSCAN ORNAMENTS IN GOLD SET WITH GARNETS; NECKLACE
AND EARRINGS

nimate nature wherewith to enhance his appearance. Ornaments of this kind date back to early prehistoric times.
Aurignac man, in the Ice Age, possessed many such ornaments.
Diluvial man of this period knew nothing of agriculture, lived
in natural caves and hunted reindeer and mammoth, yet hung
himself with ornaments in the shape of perforated shells of
Nassa reticulata strung in chains, and a male of the race
was discovered in Brunn with a necklace of six hundred fossil
razor-shells and pierced fragments of mammoth tusk.

Hornes has pointed out that the burial places of prehistoric
man show that his taste was for objects appearing to him
uncommon, surprising or odd. But his choice was not un-
influenced by the æsthetic sense and he must also have valued
form, colour and polish. There is no doubt that at an early
period peculiarities of shapes, etc., in natural objects which

157

ANCIENT ROMAN RINGS

caught his attention and prompted him to appropriate them
must have awakened in him the idea of combining these thin
to enhance their value and significance. Certain kinds
stones were scarce, the teeth and horns of certain anima
more dangerous than others to obtain, and so forth. Ment
associations of this kind no doubt led to the ascription of hidd
powers to certain objects, thus converting them into amulet
The claws of a wild beast which had been slain would come
be thought of as a protection in combat against beasts of th
same kind, while glittering stones and strangely formed she
gave birth to ideas of a superstitious nature. It is certain th
ornaments hung about the person have the closest connect
with belief in talismans and, indeed, may have first originat
in, and been determined by, that belief. Gottfried Semp
thinks it an open question whether the art of ornament ga
occasion for attaching the amulet to the body, or wheth
the conception of the talisman and the need to secure it fir
led to the æsthetic idea of ornament.

This may, perhaps, be one of the reasons why orname

ANCIENT ROMAN SIGNET-RING

158

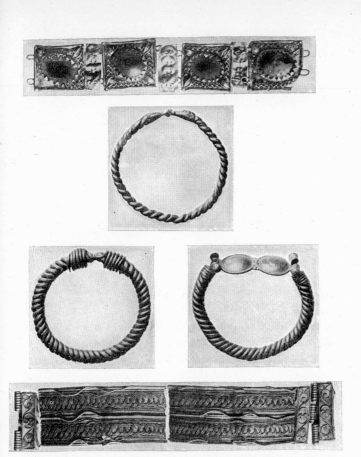

GOLD ORNAMENTS OF THE ROMAN PERIOD
Second and Third Centuries B.C.

ppears to have been the privilege of the male in the early
ages of culture; for it was the man who faced danger to
otain these objects, and again it was the man who needed
rotection, more urgently than the woman, against human
nd bestial enemies. To this day among all uncivilised
eoples the man wears more ornaments than the woman.

Among many primitive peoples in the world to-day a dis-
roportionate amount of trouble, thought and labour is spent

159

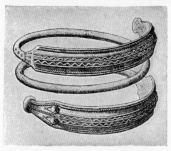
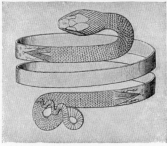

GOLD BRACELET FOUND IN SEELAND   GOLD BRACELET FOUND IN POMPEII
Copenhagen Museum   *Naples Museum*

upon the adornment of the body, and we may deduce tha
prehistoric man was very deeply concerned with the discover
of new possibilities of decoration, new materials and so forth
Excavations of prehistoric sites have revealed an extraordinar
wealth of articles of personal ornament, affording evidenc
that man's love of it must have driven him to incessar
search for new personal decorations. Even in paleolith
epochs, such as the Solutrian and Magdalenian, we find snai
shells, animals' teeth and pierced stones, while the neolith
period adds to these materials bone, flint, jet and flakes
shell. Chains and pendants to adorn the person were made
snail-shells, human teeth, fish spines, bones, ivory, ambe
jet, turquoise, jade, glass and rock-crystal. By the typ
of ornament we can estimate the advances made in huma
culture in prehistoric times. As early as the neolithic age v
find copper and gold ornaments, which increase in numb
during the copper age, while the bronze age brings in the u
of anklets, neck-rings, diadems and brooches. In the lat
bronze age, or Hallstatt age, indeed (the period, perhap
of the Trojan wars), the custom of adorning the body in the
ways seems to have reached its zenith. Silver, however, do
not appear as a material in use for ornaments till the La Tèn
period. But the love of ornament, which led to the acquir
ment of all these materials, was also active at an early dat
in working, selecting and combining them and so producin

160

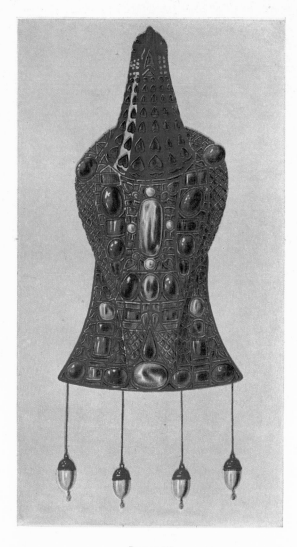

PLATE XI

LARGE FIBULA

From the West Gothic Treasure of Petrossa
Bucharest Museum

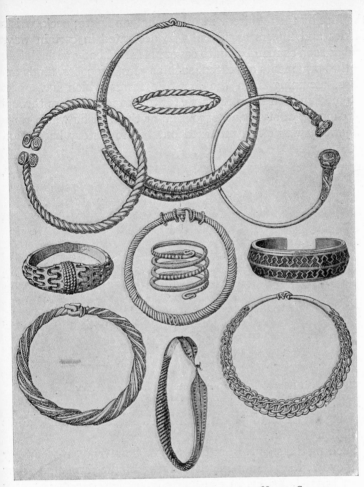

NORDIC GOLD AND SILVER ORNAMENTS, FOUND IN NORTH GERMANY, DENMARK, SWEDEN, HUNGARY, AND RUSSIA

the first real "jewelry." Man enhanced the value of his raw materials by working upon them, and in the process discovered the principle of *rhythm*, that principle which forms the very basis of all the arts.

The main types of personal ornament were determined from

the first by the requirements of the human figure; neck, wrists
ankles and fingers could only be decorated in certain ways
and as soon as man began to cover his naked body with clothes
clothes-ornaments appeared, such as pins, brooches, studs and
belts, assuming from the first the forms which have been
retained, in their main features, for thousands of years through
all changes of style and executive method. The whole range
of jewelry was clearly marked out before history began, and

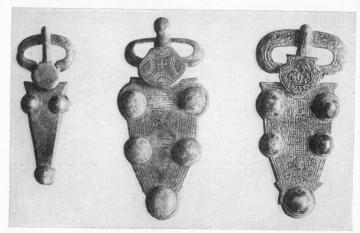

nothing was left to prehistoric man's successors, but endless
variations of the same theme.

Such pictures as remain to us show how very early jewelry
was evolved. The far-famed drawing of the *femme au renne*
from Basse-Laugerie, in the Piette collection, one of the very
earliest of all existing representations of the human figure and
dating back to the Magdalenian period, shows a woman completely naked, but wearing necklace and bracelets. Neolithic
drawings, also, show women unclad but carrying massive
ornaments on neck and breasts. The principal lesson, indeed,
of these relics of the prehistoric world is that ornaments
existed long before clothing.

The facts are confirmed by conditions found to exist among savages when the civilised world (if one may presume so to call it!) first came into contact with them. In the tropics there was far more ornament than clothing. The aboriginal Caribbees went naked, and Lippert stresses the circumstance

THE GREAT NECK-RING FROM THE WEST GOTHIC TREASURE
OF PETROSSA, IN GOLD, ENAMEL AND PRECIOUS STONES
Bucharest Museum

that they used such fabrics as they had the art to make solely for purposes of decoration at times of festivity; they wore gold ornaments, while absolutely devoid of clothing. The inhabitants of the Andamans were without protective clothing, yet travellers found that they would wear as many as twelve different sorts of necklaces, hung with coral, shells and human finger-bones. Bushmen carry an immense weight of ornaments of all kinds about their persons but wear no clothing whatsoever, and, indeed, tropical races in general, to whom it has never occurred to seek covering from the cold and

163

wet, have been found in possession of such masses of ornamen
that the contrast between the lack of what we deem a necessit
and the wealth of what we regard as superfluous has strongl
impressed all travellers. These things, however, are super
fluous only from the point of view of the modern Europea
(to avoid that very inappropriate term "civilised man"). I
prehistoric times and among primitive peoples ornament
served subsidiary ends quite as important, perhaps, as thei
proper one of adornment, though these functions have lapsee
among more advanced races. Ornaments served as currency
or, at least, were handy objects for purposes of barter in defaul
of it. To this day from the African continent to the island
of the Pacific the cowrie-shell is as good as current coin, the
value of a single shell varying from the thousandth part of a
shilling to the five-thousandth according to the exchange.
Cowrie shells had been carried to the Baltic as early as the
bronze age, and so probably served the same purpose then.
In the same way the most ancient form of metal ornament
became also the earliest form of metal coinage. The bronze
arm-rings and finger-rings of the Hallstatt period are made
very accurately in certain weights and were valid trade
currency throughout the Mediterranean lands. Of still higher
value were the golden "bauge," the big arm- and neck-rings,

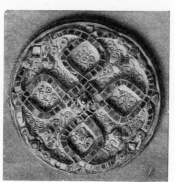

DISK-SHAPED FIBULA FROM WITTISLINGEN OF THE SEVENTH OR
EIGHTH CENTURY A.D., IN GOLD WITH HONEYCOMB GLAZING
AND FILIGREE. (*National Museum, Munich*)

164

HALF-MOON-SHAPED FIBULA WITH PENDANTS, IN GRAVEN SILVER,
OF THE HALLSTATT PERIOD, SEVENTH TO SIXTH CENTURY, B.C.
FOUND IN CARNIOLA. (*Antiquarium, Munich*)

which, down to historic times, were coveted by both kings and
subjects, warriors and minstrels. They were made in certain
weights and were good as current coin. This led very early
to their being "faked"; they would be cast hollow and then
filled with lead, or else made of solid copper and thinly gilded.
Clara Schumann once complained to Brahms that a certain
bracelet given her by a princess was so old-fashioned that she
could not wear it, but when she came to sell it it appeared that
the gold was thin as paper and the underlying substance was
tin. Simple soul! It is clear that this particular trick was
ancient even in ancient times.

Connected with the use of ornaments as money is the
Sumatra custom of loading bride and bridesmaids at a wedding
with heavy metal rings, thus displaying the amount of the
dowry to all beholders, and Selenka records that he saw a
Malay bride wearing gold ornaments to the value of about
four hundred pounds as part of her purchase money. Hindus

c. A.D. 1000

EARRINGS FROM THE EMPRESS GISELA'S TREASURE

and Tamils, even the poorer classes, overload themselves with silver ornaments, which represent all their wealth and, being worn on their bodies, are comparatively safe from thieves. The luxurious display of personal ornament in the early Middle Ages and even as late as the Renaissance is largely explained by the fact that opportunities for investing capital in trade were lacking, while gold ornaments and jewels were a form of investment which could at any moment be converted into ready money.

Another ancillary use of ornament was the symbolic; it

c. A.D. 1000

BROOCH FROM THE EMPRESS
GISELA'S TREASURE

166

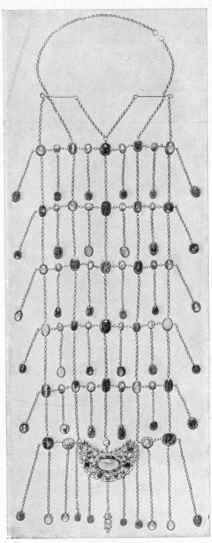

GOLD NECKLACE, WITH GEMS AND PEARLS FROM THE
EMPRESS GISELA'S TREASURE

c. A.D. 1000. *Palace Museum, Berlin*

167

witnessed to the rank and riches of him who wore it, and
in certain circumstances, to his physical strength and courage
also. When the bold and skilful hunter hung roung his neck
the teeth of the wild beast he had slain, he thereby decorated
himself with an Order which proclaimed his service to the
community in quite unmistakable fashion. In New Guinea
the natives make themselves armlets from the lower jaw-
bones of defeated enemies, while the Appalachian Indians wore

CORONATION ARMLET OF THE GERMAN EMPERORS
Twelfth Century

necklaces of dried human finger-bones. Savage peoples in
South America preserve and prepare the heads of their slain
enemies till they become small and shrunken and then hang
them about their necks. In these instances the ornament, in
its secondary use, becomes not only an emblem of prowess,
but also an amulet.

The connection between ornament and amulet is so close
that many investigators seek to explain primitive man's desire for ornament wholly by his wish to possess an amulet as
an effective means of protection against supernatural powers.
However that may be, this sort of significance certainly remained

168

herent in ornament into historic times and exists to-day in
the charms which many superstitious persons carry on watch-
chains or elsewhere about them. The breast-plate of the High
Priest of the ancient Hebrews which, by means of twelve
stones set in gold, the Urim and Thummim, represented the
twelve tribes of Israel, was a talisman, and it is to the *stone*
lore particularly and the magic power ascribed to it that
superstition has always clung with the greatest persistence—

COVER OF A POCKET MIRROR IN IVORY, REPRE-
SENTING THE STORMING OF THE CASTLE OF LOVE
Fifteenth Century

persistence, indeed, almost strong enough to make one waver
into belief in some actual hidden power. When, during the
seventh century B.C., the Greeks first came to know of precious
stones (no doubt by way of the East) they also adopted the
already existent belief in their magic properties. This belief
linked precious stones with the planets and the seasons; the
twelve months corresponded to the so-called "stones of the
zodiac," one for each month, and some people wore in January
a jacinth, in February an amethyst, in March a jasper, in April
a sapphire, in May an agate, in June an emerald, in July an
onyx, in August a cornelian, in September a chrysolite, in

October a beryl, in November a topaz, and in December
ruby. Others adopted the emerald for May, the chalcedon
for June, the cornelian for July, the sardonyx for August, th
aquamarine for October, for December chrysoprase, turquoi
or malachite.

In the Christian era symbolic significance was transferre
to the "apostle stones," twelve to represent the twelve apostle
jasper for St. Peter, sapphire for St. Andrew, chalcedony fo

GOLD HELMET OF DUKE CHARLES THE
BOLD OF BURGUNDY, SET WITH PEARLS
AND PRECIOUS STONES

St. James, emerald for St. John, sardonyx for St. Philip
cornelian for St. Bartholomew, chrysolite for St. Matthew
beryl for St. Thomas, chrysoprase for St. Thaddæus, topa
for St. James the Less, jacinth for St. Simon and amethys
for St. Matthias. In the late Middle Ages people still believe
in the protective and healing properties of precious stones an
their magic effect when worn upon the finger. The ruby gav
peace of mind and serenity of soul, the sapphire heavenl
happiness, the emerald earthly prosperity, the chalcedon
victorious power and health, the diamond protection agains
outward foes. Dietrich von Glatz possessed a magic girdl

170

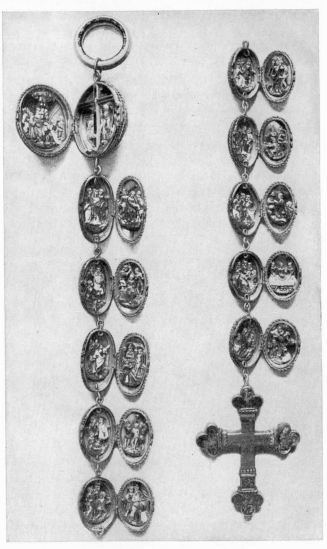

ROSARY IN AGATES AND GOLD ENAMEL
French work of the Sixteenth Century (Louvre)

171

decorated with gold and set with more than fifty precious stones, to ensure honour and happiness, respect, victory and invulnerability.

In the Middle Ages the stone-cutter's art was lost, and antique cameos and intaglios were very highly prized; the manner of their making was a mystery and occult powers were attributed to them. For example, stones cut with the figure of Pegasus were considered to be a remarkably efficacious protection to horses. The emerald was believed to be good for the eyes, the ruby protected the wearer from poverty, the amethyst from the evil consequence of drunkenness, while corals were a remedy for hemorrhage. In an age when the rich and powerful lived in constant fear of poison, objects supposed to be antidotes were eagerly sought after. Of these the unicorn horn was held to be the most potent, but in default of this the stomach- and gall-stones of certain animals were used under the name of bezoars and were often set in costly fashion. Elk-hooves were worn for protection against epilepsy and tongues of asps (which were really sharks' teeth) against the bites of poisonous snakes. When the Germanic peoples became converts to Christianity, they chose pendants in the form of the cross as the most efficacious of all amulets. The superstition of astrology, which reached its zenith in the sixteenth and seventeenth centuries, brought to the fore talismans engraved with astrological signs and inscriptions, the more unintelligible the better.

Following the development of ornament through the centuries, it becomes apparent that whenever man acquired some fresh knowledge of material and technical skill he forthwith employed them in fashioning his ornaments. This began in the stone age when nomadic man, a hunter and a warrior, used to this end whatever natural objects chance brought in his way, objects upon which, for the most part, he could not work at all, except perhaps by boring holes through them. Yet finds of amber dating from remote times show that even then barter was carried on, at least in articles of personal adornment. As soon as his tools were equal to the task man began

o work upon his findings, such as teeth and antlers, which
e had hitherto been obliged to use in their rough state.

The greatest forward step, and one which was to have the
most influence on future developments, was taken in the
ronze age. The use of metals first made it possible for body
rnaments to become actual works of art, neck-, arm-, and
nger-rings taking the place of unshaped objects of adorn-

Lucas Cranach   1529

PORTRAIT OF THE ELECTOR JOACHIM I
OF BRANDENBURG
Old Pinakothek, Munich

nent. The craft of the metal-worker included casting, refining,
graving and embossing, and all were employed in the fashion-
g of decorations. Man's love of ornament was thereby sub-
antially enhanced and reached a high-water mark in the
allstatt period. Riveting was then understood, though not
ldering nor gilding. Finds of coral and beads show that there
as already a certain amount of trade. This period added the
bula and the earring to the already existing forms of ornament.

173

Then, too, appeared jingling ornaments, little thin plates of bronze strung upon small chains which were attached to the belt or to some part of the clothing so that they rang or rattled with every movement of the wearer. It has been surmised that they served to distinguish women of rank, and they were used over a very long period. In the early days of German history women wore little jingling ornaments attached to their ear

THE ELECTRESS MAGDALENA OF BRANDENBURG, FIRST CONSORT OF JOACHIM II, WITH A COIF OF PEARLS, COLLAR, NECKLACE AND PENDANT
After a painting in the Hohenzollern Museum, Berlin

rings, a form of jewelry much used by many different races at varying levels of culture. It is known to have existed in ancient Mexico, and in India to this day the women wear hollow anklets containing small pebbles for the sake of the tinkling sound they give.

The succeeding, the so-called La Tène era, was the age of Celtic culture and brings us to the pre-Roman iron age and to two new inventions of importance to the jeweller's craft namely wrought-metal chains and the earliest form of enamel

174

rade was active, the glass industry had attained a high degree
i perfection in Egypt, where blue or patterned arm-rings
ere made, apparently for export purposes. In shape they
ere copies of the La Tène arm-rings and must have been
oveted ornaments in Gaul and southern Germany, though
oubtless only obtainable by the rich, for in the first century

THE ELECTRESS HEDWIG OF BRANDENBURG, SECOND
CONSORT OF JOACHIM II, WITH A COIF OF PEARLS AND
TWO NECKLACES

After a painting in the Hohenzollern Museum, Berlin

.c. they are found only in the graves of women whose burial
laces show them to have been persons of rank.

The Celtic civilisation, having its headquarters in Gaul,
ows the enamel-worker's craft brought to a very high level.
lthough these peoples imported certain ornaments, they
xported others in considerable quantities. The device of
ving brightness and interest to metal ornaments by inlaying
oloured material was practised by the Germanic races at a
eriod before history gives any account of them. The earliest

175

form was an inlay of coloured glass held in place by strips o
metal, the patterns being usually geometrical. The wor
was effective in itself and not difficult to carry out, qualitie
which ensured for it long continuance. At a later period glas
gave way to semi-precious stones, such as almandines an
garnets. This inlay work came originally from the East an

NECKLACE OF QUEEN CLAUDIA OF FRANCE, CONSORT
OF FRANCIS I (1530)

made its way westwards. It was known in Egypt from th
earliest times. The craft of enamelling, which took the plac
of tarsia-work in stone, was also known to the Egyptian
It reached its zenith at the close of the tenth century of th
Christian era in Byzantium, where coloured enamels attaine
a variety, a brilliance and a transparency which has never bee
surpassed. *Cloisonné*, in which applied fillets of metal separat
the various coloured enamel pastes, came to be distinguishe
from *champlevé*, in which the graving tool was used to cu

176

PLATE XII

GOLD CHAIN AND PENDANT ENAMELLED AND SET WITH
RUBIES AND PEARLS

From the portrait of a Princess, early 17th Century, in the Worlitz Gallery,

By permission of E. Wasmuth & Co., Publishers, Berlin

Lucas Cranach

PORTRAIT OF A YOUNG LADY

Germanic Museum, Nuremberg

ollows in the metal background for the same purpose. The
articular use of enamel for which Limoges became famous
d not appear till the sixteenth century.

Pierced stones strung in chains have been found in the very
dest burial grounds, but it was not till comparatively late
at any attempt was made to combine stones and metal in
single ornament; considerable technical understanding of
oth materials had first to be acquired.   Stones could only be
olished, and that upon their natural surfaces, for the method
cutting facets is quite modern.   On the other hand the art
cutting pictures in the face of the stone is of great antiquity.
derives from Babylon where such *intaglios* were used as
gnets, or hung about the neck as amulets.   Under the fourth
gyptian dynasty the scarab appears on signet stones.   This
istom took a long time to reach the Greeks.   Homer mentions
either finger-rings, precious stones nor seals.   Finger-rings,
deed, were unknown in Greece until after the Persian wars,

N

WATCHES. *Sixteenth Century*

but that artistic race brought the craft of cutting stone to degree of perfection which, though it might possibly be equalle in later ages, could never be surpassed. To the art of incisin stone, the art of *intaglio*, they also added that of working i relief, that is of *cameo*.

At first in Greece the wearing of a ring with a carved ston inset was a sign of rank, but when Herodotus wrote that every one in Babylon, of whatever standing, had his signet-ring the fashion spread among all classes of Hellenes. The signe ring served as a token, taking the place of written credential for ambassadors and messengers. The use of the carved ston as a seal was not practised in Rome till the last decade of th Republic, and though, according to Livy, the Sabines had wor signet-rings in the days of Romulus, they were, like those o the Romans, made solely of metal. In ancient Rome ever man wore a simple iron signet-ring, though later these wer frequently replaced by gold rings. At first these latter wer

178

WATCHES. *Sixteenth Century*

the privilege of the *nobiles*, then the *equites* adopted their use and finally they were worn by all and sundry, even by women. The stone-set ring no sooner appeared in Rome than it became another item in the ever-increasing tale of luxury. It was fashionable to wear more than one at a time, and later they came to be worn on every finger (Martial jests at

179

Charinus for having six on each finger) and were changed with the seasons of the year. Under the Empire a gold ring bearing the emperor's picture, when bestowed by the emperor, gave the possessor the right to approach the august presence unannounced.

Except in rings the Greeks did not use gems and gold in combination, a restraint practised also by neighbouring peoples of allied culture. The Phœnicians strung pieces of amber in

WATCHES. *Sixteenth Century*

chains, Egyptians made necklaces of cornelian, lapis lazuli, green felspar, coral, shells, porcelain, etc., and Cretans made chains of the so-called "island stone," but in early days combination of the two elements of jewelry was not attempted. It was under the emperors that Roman society first became acquainted with precious stones, which were brought in great numbers and variety from India to the capital city of the ancient world. Roman ladies made great display with them; the red and white sardonyx, the onyx, amethyst, jacinth, sapphire,

hrysolite, topaz, turquoise, beryl, emerald and opal were
reatly coveted and high prices were paid for them. The
mpress Lollia Paulina is said to have worn every day emeralds
nd pearls worth many thousands. The men, however, were
ot to be outdone by the women, and the senator Nonius
ossessed a ring set with an opal for which he is reputed to
ave paid a sum approximating to eight thousand pounds.

WATCHES. *Sixteenth Century*

Gold ornaments were very highly prized in Greece, a con-
butory cause, no doubt, being the fact that that country
ill-supplied with the precious metal and had to import it.
wealth of gold ornaments has been found in the second
lony in Hissarlik, discovered by Schliemann, identified by
m with the Homeric Troy, and estimated to date from about
oo to 1500 years before Christ. Fine artistry and immense
our must have been expended in making these ornaments;
e famous diadem or necklace reconstructed by Schliemann
nsists of 90 chains, 12,271 rings, 4,066 leaves, and 16 pendants,
in pure gold.

The characteristic Ionic goldsmith-work attained its zenith about the fifth or fourth century B.C. Specimens of this work exhibit an advanced culture and a high standard of taste for it is quite clear that the aim was to get effect by small

WATCHES FROM THE TREASURY OF THE IMPERIAL
HOUSE OF AUSTRIA

That in the right-hand bottom corner, in a Case cut out of a Single Emerald, belonged to Marie Antoinette

pieces of exquisite workmanship and not by a mere mass ornament hung upon the person. The material is never allowed to be obtrusive but takes second place to craftsmanship nevertheless the treatment, in which filigree and granulation are employed, suits the precious metal most admirably, and

182

Above: CHATELAINE WITH WATCH AND BERLOQUES (*design by P. Moreau, Paris, 1771*). *Below:* FRONT AND BACK VIEW OF A CHATELAINE AND WATCH (*design by Maria, Paris, c. 1765*)

grace in conception is most happily united with delicacy in execution. These earrings, hair-pins, necklaces and bracelets were certainly not designed for effect at a distance, for the fine workmanship requires close scrutiny to display its beauties. In the Greek colonies on the Black Sea, where Greek culture came into contact with backward and half-savage peoples a barbaric element in taste is unmistakable.

Greek ornaments are almost all body-ornaments; the fibula was used to fasten clothes but girdles were not worn. In contrast to this the Cretan-Mycenæan culture appears to have preferred dress ornaments, and, judging by finds in graves to have used them in considerable numbers. Their garment would seem to have been over-decorated with a mass of thinly hammered gold plates, embossed with naturalistic designs. The Greeks of Byzantine times revived this form of ornament but those of the classical period would have none of it.

Grecian style in ornament exercised a most fortunate influence upon the Etruscans, whose culture flourished between the eighth and the fourth century before Christ. The Etruscan must have been a jewelry-loving people with special delight in polished metal. They were most excellent workers in gold and understood casting, refining, embossing, soldering engraving, filigree work and enamel. They worked in gold as thin as paper, though probably only for burial with their dead, for no living men and women could ever have worn without damaging them, those marvellous wreaths in gold leaf, imitating olive, laurel, oak, and myrtle with an astonishing fidelity to nature; only the peace of the grave could have preserved them intact. Yet living men and women must have worn much jewelry; arms, shoulders, breast, neck and fingers were adorned with pendants, rings, clasps, etc. The amulet worn about the neck in the form of a *bulla* clearly played an important part. After the year 295 B.C. Etruria became Roman and imparted aspects of its culture to Rome. The Romans, their cult of simplicity and abhorrence of luxury notwithstanding, went in for goldsmith's work even in the days of Numa. They probably borrowed the *bulla*, and indeed

184

he whole conception of the amulet, from the Etruscans, for
ven in the days of the Republic their world-wide conquests
rought them into contact with the habits and customs of
distant peoples, by all of whom they were influenced.

Rome being chiefly a military state, expended its inventive
ower in the matter of ornament mainly on its soldiers, and

GOLD AND ENAMEL WATCHES

t is to Rome that the world owes "decorations" and "orders."
The earliest distinction for bravery was the silver arm-ring,
he *galbeus*, which was bestowed on her warriors—as freely as
certain modern decorations, it would appear, for one Licinius
Dentatus acquired a hundred and sixty of them. Next came
he *phaleræ*, disk-like medals to hang upon the breast, for the
cavalry, and to these two "orders" the Empire added the neck-
ring, the *torques*, probably copied from the Celts. Tomb-
stones of Roman centurions have been found with records

185

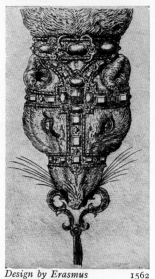

Design by Erasmus   1562
Hornig, of Nuremberg

HEAD OF A FUR COLLAR

of decorations actually numerou
enough to put even the higher com
mand of the late régime in German
into the shade!

Roman ornament is heavier i
style than Grecian, and in the tim
of the migrations became positivel
coarse, for the barbarians, accus
tomed during their wanderings t
carry their entire wealth on thei
backs, were far more impressed b
sheer massiveness in gold than b
skilled craftsmanship in ornament
Byzantium, the political heir o
Rome, adopted nevertheless unde
Eastern influences an entirely different style in ornament and develope
the bedizening of the garment rathe
than of the person to excess. Robe

were literally covered with gold,
gems, metal and enamel plaques,
and it is a mystery how the
Emperor and Empress moved at
all in their bejewelled garments;
it must have been utterly impossible for them to sit down. These
two tendencies, the inclination to
the massive, and the preference
for lavish adornment of the dress,
dominated the taste of the northern
peoples for centuries after the fall
of Rome.

Among the Germans, men as
well as women wore purely de-
corative pieces of jewelry, of no
practical value beyond the worth
of the metal of which they were

Design by Benvenuto Cellini (?)

PENDANT IN GOLD AND ENAMEL
WITH PRECIOUS STONES AND PEARLS

186

ade, besides other ornaments
esigned to some particular end.
Their burial places yield examples
f this in bronze, silver and
ven in tin, as well as in gold.
Of these ornaments the most
ncient is the plain neck-ring,
vorn by Germans and Celts alike,
nd which, as we have seen, gave
he Romans the idea for their
nost distinguished military de-
oration. These rings were smooth,
piral or grooved; in early days,
f course, they were without
tones and we learn for the first
ime in *Beowulf* of one set with
a stone which was the property
f a king and was used on occa-
.ions of special magnificence. The
neck-ring was sometimes shaped
ike a collar, wide in the middle
and narrowing towards either

Erasmus Hornig   Nuremberg, 1562
DESIGN FOR A PENDANT

nd, and occasionally it was triple, like a modern pearl neck-
ace. Specimens of Gothic goldsmith's-work survive from the

Design by Hans Holbein
From Luthmer's
Goldschmuck der Renaissance

PENDANT IN GOLD,
DIAMONDS, AND PEARLS

fourteenth century, with garnet mosaic.
The *Heliand* mentions neck-rings set with
pearls and precious stones such as are also
described in the *Ruodlieb*. After Pagan
times the neck-ring became rarer among
men though the arm-ring long persisted.

The arm-ring, or "bauge," was among the
most frequently worn of ornaments and its
use reaches far back into prehistoric times.
Pliny finds it characteristic of the Celts, and
the ambitions of Germanic heroes were
focussed upon the golden arm-ring. Indeed
the Old-Saxon name for a prince was "Ring-

187

1560

GOLD AND ENAMEL NECKLACE FROM THE TREASURY OF DUKE ALBERT V
OF BAVARIA. Miniature by H. Mülich. (*National Museum, Munich*)

spender," the "ring-dispenser." It was the duty of great
lords by virtue of their rank to dispense these rings to their
guests and followers, and their treasuries must often have
contained them by the hundred. When Walter of Aquitaine
fled from Attila, King of the Huns, he took with him so many
arm-rings from that monarch's treasury that he was able to
give King Gunther no less than a hundred of them. Siegfried,
coming to Worms to tell the court of the arrival of Gunther
and Brunhild, demanded a messenger's reward and received
twenty-four arm-rings from Kriemhild. When leaving
Bechelaere the Margravine Gotelind slipped twelve arm-
rings over the hand of Volker the bard. A certain sanctity
attached to the arm-ring; friends exchanged them as pledges,

1560

GOLD AND ENAMEL NECKLACE FROM THE TREASURY OF DUKE ALBERT V
OF BAVARIA. Miniature by H. Mülich. (*National Museum, Munich*)

188

aths were sworn upon them and they were given as offerings
o the gods. The heathen priest in the exercise of his office
ore a ring upon his arm. Kings who, as we should say to-day,
anted a "good press," that is to say, were anxious that the
ards should sing their renown, made a point of being lavish
the bestowal of arm-rings. Thus Waylandsmith had
make not only swords but also arm-rings for King Neithardt.

Adriaen Grabeth   *Munich*
PORTRAIT

he *Hildebrandslied, Heliand* and *Beowulf* treat of these orna-
ents and even Charlemagne wore them upon his upper
m. King Conrad I on his death-bed commanded the crown
wels to be delivered to King Henry I, among them being
m-rings which remained part of the German insignia down
the middle of the twelfth century. Even in the thirteenth
ntury minnesingers describe men's armlets, but as that
ntury drew to a close they finally disappeared, probably
sted by the prevalent fashion for the long-sleeved robe.

189

After the neck-ring and the arm ring, the finger-ring was the mo frequently used form of ornamen even the poorest appear to hav worn it. The oldest specimens a made of bent wire, often so wid however, as to cover a whole join But there is an almost endle variety of both shapes and materia Gold is frequent, silver rare, and w find also brass, copper, tin and iro for according to the old ecclesiastic rule the man should wear a gold, th woman a silver or iron betroth ring. Neidhardt speaks of rings mad of plaited hair. Peasants' rings we often made of tin-plated lead set with a paste sapphir imitation pearls were made of fishes, eyes and rings we formed of glass, a craft known in the days of Theophil Presbyter. The old rings were clumsy affairs; Charles th Bold's signet-ring weighed half a pound.

Dress ornaments were influenced by Byzantine styles. Angilbert relates that Charlemagne's daughter wore mantles decorated with gold plates and precious stones. In the *Nibelungenlied* Brunhild wears such garments and in the *Wigalois* a mantle is described as similarly adorned. Garments were trimmed with borders stitched in gold and studded with gems; from the eleventh century they were also set with little silver bells, a bizarre fashion that lasted till the fifteenth century. The oldest accredited specimen in this style is the coronation robe of Emperor Otto III,

hich was adorned with three hundred and fifty-five little
olden bells in the shape of pomegranates; the Emperor pre-
nted the garment to the church of Ara Cœli in Rome. Bells
ere sewn on the hems of every type of garment, on the
ip, the toe of the shoe, the helmet, the spurs. They became
regular part of the costume of the upper classes in Germany.
lrich von Liechtenstein relates that Herr Illsung von Scheuf-

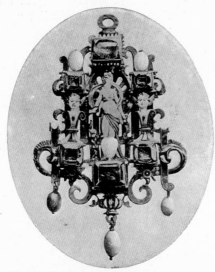

After the School of Hans Mülich　　　　*c.* 1550

GOLD PENDANT, ENAMELLED WITH PRECIOUS
STONES AND PEARLS SURROUNDING A FIGURE
OF CLEOPATRA. (*British Museum, London*)

:h, with whom he broke a lance, rode out to meet him with
ve hundred bells upon his person.
The most important dress ornament was, however, the
rdle, and upon it was lavished almost incredible magnificence.
he wife of King Philip the Tall of France wore at her corona-
on a golden girdle set with rubies and emeralds. In 1166
e Margravine Kunigunde of Steiermark bought a manor on
e Fischach, paying for it by means of a girdle, of the weight
one gold mark, set with sixty ells of pearls. Étienne de

Hans Mülich (?)

GOLD PENDANT TO THE
GRAND COLLAR OF THE
ORDER OF ST. MICHAEL
(*The Treasury, Munich*)

Bourbon declaimed passionately against
this form of luxury, especially in regard
to the elaborate workmanship which was
even more expensive than the materials.
The gold plates of which many of these
belts were made were chased or embossed
with figures of lions, dragons, birds and
the like, and it was with an allusion to
these that the moralist prophesied that
"those who wear these girdles shall the
lions and dragons of hell one day devour."
Perhaps the singers who have described
these marvels have sometimes drawn
rather a long bow. In the *Meleranz von
dem Pleier* we are told of a belt with
an inscription upon it done all in precious
stones.

Both sexes wore the belt, and both
used brooches to fasten their garments.
The fibula, indeed, is among the oldest of ornaments; it
was indispensable when man first began to wear clothes and
it has been one of the most generally used articles in all
ages since. It might go by different names, it might change
in style, but to this day, in the form of the brooch, it is as
popular as it was thousands of years ago. It can scarcely be
claimed that progress has been made in the construction of
this "safety-pin," though at different periods more care or
less has been expended upon its ornamentation. At first it
was often shaped like some fantastic animal, and the art of
Germanic peoples long gave free play to fancy and employed
every new technical or æsthetic advance in beautifying the
fibula. Between the fourth and the sixth century, when Gothic
goldsmiths still dominated the Germanic craft, the fibula
reached its zenith. One incomparable specimen has been
found in a man's grave at Wittislingen, near Lauingen, a
large clasp-pin cast in silver and gilded, inlaid with enamel
work, with filigree work, set with almandines, and green paste

192

PLATE XIII

GOLD PENDANTS
Enamelled, with precious stones, pearls and cameos
16th Century

"Bijouteries" in Gold and Enamel with large Pearls
Sixteenth Century. Imperial Treasury, Vienna

n reticulated gold-foil; its date is probably about A.D. 600
n inscription on the under side states that Uffila has had this
bula made in memory of his dead wife, and one Wigerig, also
amed, is thought by Bassermann-Jordan to have been the
oldsmith. The sorrowing widower who had a resplendent
wel made to comfort him for the loss of his wife must have
een a man of sensibility.

After the twelfth century the mantle was usually fastened,
ot on the shoulder as formerly, but on the breast, and the
asp which held it became larger and usually disk-shaped.
oets exerted themselves to describe its beauties, and Wirnt
on Gravenberg sings of a brooch set with a carbuncle as large
s a bean. It was not long before the brooch gave place to
nother device. Instead of a single ornament, one was fastened
t either edge of the mantle in front; these were called in old
rench "tassels" and were joined by a cord which was made
st to one "tassel" and could be pulled loose or tight through
e other. The mode being French it was secure of the approval

o

of the fashionable. The "tassels" were frequently made of gold set with gems and chased or embossed with designs of birds, flowers, etc. In the *Meleranz* two "tassels" are described in detail; one showed Venus with a torch, the other Cupid with bow and arrows. Particularly pious ladies would join their "tassels" with a rosary instead of a cord.

Both sexes generally wore the same kinds of ornament, though those worn by men were perhaps rather heavier and more solid. Women alone, however, wore earrings, which were not adopted in Germany till a comparatively late period, and even then were speedily condemned to long disuse by the prevailing fashions in hairdressing which completely hid the ears. The wearing of rings through pierced lobes of the ear was originally an oriental custom and did not reach the Greeks and Romans till the time of the migrations; in the Hallstatt era it was unknown. The Celts were the first of the northern races to adopt the fashion and earrings were much worn by women in Gaul under the Merovingian dynasty. Among the Germanic tribes also it was an imported and not an indigenous custom, for whenever it is mentioned in medieval documents it is always with some such explanatory phrase as "such as the Italians" or "as the Slavs are wont to wear." Nevertheless earrings found in women's graves in Germany are among the most beautiful and tasteful examples of German craftsmanship extant.

From the twelfth to the seventeenth century mirrors played a conspicuous role as objects of virtu. Both the hand-mirror and the pocket-mirror are forms of great antiquity. The earliest surviving specimen is, in Forrer's opinion, a hand-mirror, adapted also for hanging, which was found in a lake dwelling at Port Alban on Lake Neuchâtel; it is oval with a spiral bronze handle ending in a ring and the back is decorated with a zigzag pattern. A circular bronze mirror with a broken handle and engraved designs found by Montelius in an early Etruscan grave at the Arnoldi burial-grounds is probably the next oldest specimen.

In early historic times the hand-mirror continued to be made

194

Above: Gold Pendant Trophy in the form of the Arms of the Order of the Knights of St. John, made of Two Hundred and Forty-Five Precious Stones and Six Pear-shaped Pearls. 1603.

Right: Gold Pendant in Brown Enamel with Precious Stones, Rubies and Pearls, Sixteenth Century

Left: Gold Pendant with Cameo of Duke Philip III. of Burgundy, cut in Chalcedony

All in the Treasury, Munich

195

PENDANT TO A GOLD FILIGREE
CHAIN, ENAMELLED
Munich work of the Sixteenth Century

GOLD PENDANT, ENAMELLED, WITH
DIAMONDS, RUBIES, EMERALDS AND
PEARLS SURROUNDING A FIGURE
OF CHARITY
*German work of the Sixteenth Century
British Museum*

of metal. The Egyptians used copper and the Jews adopted
this method from them. When Moses wished to make brazen
vessels for the tabernacle, he compelled the women of Israel
to surrender their hand-mirrors for the purpose. The manufacture of mirrors seems to have been a thriving industry
among the Etruscans and Romans. Both used every sort of
metal that would take a polish, and the Etruscans employed
a bronze 19 to 32 per cent richer in tin than the usual bronze
of antiquity. The Romans used to overlay the surface of
the mirror with silver, though by the time of Pompey gold had
taken the place of silver, which was actually despised, the very
maid-servants insisting on gold for their mirrors.

Even in antiquity small glass mirrors existed as well as
metal reflectors. They were known in Egypt a century before
the Christian era and Pliny tells us that the best were reputed
to be made in Sidon. A large number have been found in
Roman graves in south and west Germany, on the Rhine,

196

near Regensburg and at Saalburg. Isidore of Seville writes
of them in the seventh century. Technical methods, however,
remained primitive enough. The mirror was cut from glass
balls filled with lead or tin, and the mirror surface probably
had no better back than resin or pitch, so that the reflection
must have been very imperfect. The very names in use at
that time bear witness to this; the Gothic "skugwa," the Old
Nordic expression "Schattensehe" (shadow-seeing), and the
Old High German "Schattengesicht" (shadow-face), all in
use for the mirror, show that human vanity was none too well
served. These technical inadequacies caused people to fall
back again on metal. The mirror given by St. Boniface to
Queen Ethelburga of Mercia was of silver. Arabic textbooks
of about A.D. 1000 mention none but mirrors of silver or steel,
and when the author of the second *Titurel* writes of a place where
mirrors were made he bluntly calls it a "mirror-smithy."

The date of the reappearance of the glass mirror is somewhat
uncertain. Theophilus Presbyter, writing of the various uses
of glass in the eleventh and early twelfth centuries, makes

GOLD PENDANT, ENAMELLED,
WITH DIAMONDS, RUBIES, AND
PEARLS, SURROUNDING FIGURES
OF VENUS AND CUPID

German Work of the Sixteenth
Century, possibly from Munich
British Museum, London

PENDANT WITH A LARGE
RUBY, CALLED "LA CÔTE
DE BRETAGNE," MADE
FOR MARY STUART

Louvre, Paris

no mention of mirrors. In 1267 Roger Bacon treats only of bronze or silver mirrors, whereas Vincent de Beauvais, writing in 1254, mentions the process of making mirrors by pouring lead on a hot plate of glass. Mirrors were certainly made at Murano near Venice by this method in 1308, and very probably still earlier.

Since the technique of those days was only adequate to the blowing of very small plates of glass, the size of the mirror was much restricted for some centuries. It seems seldom to have been larger than a florin piece. Women wore little round hand-mirrors as ornaments about their necks or attached to their girdles. Men used them no less, and Neidhardt von Reuenthal actually tells of a sword with a mirror set in the hilt. They were always ornately mounted, and it may have been their small size that led to their being so resplendently set. Piers Gaveston,

GOLD CHAINS AND PENDANTS, ENAMELLED, WITH PRECIOUS STONES AND PEARLS
Sixteenth and Seventeenth Centuries

SMALL PENDANTS WITH CAMEOS AND ENAMELS
Sixteenth and Seventeenth Centuries

King Edward II of England's ill-starred favourite, possessed in 1313 an enamelled silver mirror. An inventory taken in 1368 of the treasures of Duke Louis I of Anjou describes a little round gold mirror, made to open and shut, and attached to a gold chain and whistle. Charles II of France, on his death in 1380, left a number of valuable pocket-mirrors, among them one in gold set with four sapphires and thirty-four pearls. In 1400, when the French reclaimed Queen Isabel's dowry from the English, two little gold mirrors are particularly mentioned. In 1448 the good King René gave the wife of the seneschal of Anjou a gold mirror for which he paid a German goldsmith, Hennequin, thirty-five florins, a price representing a small fortune in present-day money.

Pictorial decorations conformed to the range of medieval taste and we have not only such representations as the twelve signs of the zodiac, Narcissus at the well and Susanna at the bath, but also Christ with the triple crown, the Madonna and Child, St. Veronica, St. Catherine, etc. St. Elizabeth, Landgravine of Thuringia, gave her husband a little ivory mirror with a picture of the Crucifixion on the back. Illustrations of themes sung by troubadours were, however, particularly beloved, and over and over again we see the "Castle of Love" attacked by knights and defended by its garrison of beautiful women. An early French example, dating from the thirteenth century, is in the Imperial Museum, Vienna, and similar specimens are to be seen in the Louvre and the Musée Cluny.

200

NECKLACE AND PENDANT IN GOLD-ENAMEL
German Work of the Sixteenth Century.   Louvre, Paris

In the Bourgeois collection, Cologne, (now dispersed) was
small French ivory hand-mirror of the fourteenth centur
showing six scenes from the *Roman de la Rose*. The Jubin
collection contained a little mirror of Italian origin with th
inscription "Di me non ti doler Donna giamai Che ben ti rene
quel che tu mi dai." "Make no complaint against me, lady.
only render back what you give me!"

The use of the pocket-mirror as an ornament was by

THE SO-CALLED "LYTE JEWEL," GOLD MEDALLION ENAMELLED, WITH
TWENTY-FIVE TABLE-CUT STONES AND FOUR ROSE-CUT STONES, SURROUND-
ING A MINIATURE OF KING JAMES I OF ENGLAND (*painted by Isaac Oliver,
or Nicholas Hilliard. Presented by the King to Thomas Lyte of Lyte's Cary,
Somerset. Waddesdon Bequest, British Museum, London*)

means confined to women of high rank. Neidhardt v
Reuenthal tells us that peasant girls carried mirrors in t
dance and that he himself gave his mistress, Friederun,
beautiful pendant mirror, which was, however, immediat
stolen from her. Men, too, did not disdain the pocket-mirr
even if, as we learn of the Duc de Berry in 1416, they carr
it concealed in a silk case. In 1510 King Ferdinand of Cas
actually raised the mirror to the status of a decoration
founding the Knightly Order of the Mirror of the Bles

202

gin in commemoration of a victory over the Moors.   This
der was, however, soon forgotten.

The mirror remained long in favour as an ornament.   "Crazy
an," mother of the Emperor Charles V, had three mirrors,
 framed in gold, decorated with emeralds and set with
quoises. The Archduchess Margaret, Regent of the Nether-
ds and daughter of the Emperor Maximilian I, an inventory
 whose possessions was taken after her death in 1530,
ned a number of mirrors in gold and silver-gilt (and one
a setting of jet, presumably for wear with mourning), all

with hairbrushes attached and adapted for hanging on t
girdle—the first of such toilet compendia of which we ha
record. In the mid-sixteenth century a new fashion came
of disguising the pocket-mirror as a little book, looking,
the uninitiated, like a prayer-book, or note-book. A mirr

BROOCH OF MARIA DE' MEDICI, QUEEN OF FRANCE.
CAMEOS, TABLE-CUT STONES AND PEARLS

concealed in "a little book with an embroidered cover" v
found among the possessions of Anna, "Queen of the Roman
consort of the future Emperor Maximilian II, on her de:
in 1547. The exquisites at the court of King Henry III
France carried their mirrors in book form in their right-ha
breeches pockets. Even so they were expensively got
Queen Margaret of Spain, wife of King Philip III, had a pock

NECK ORNAMENT IN GOLD AND ENAMEL, SET WITH PRECIOUS
STONES AND PEARLS (*after a painting by de Witte of the Countess
Palatine Magdalena, c. 1610. Schleissheim Gallery*). *From
Luthmer's "Goldschmuck der Renaissance," published by E. Was-
muth, Berlin*

mirror in a book-cover set in enamelled gold, and estimated
n 1611 to be worth sixty ducats.

The pocket-mirror remained an essential part of the full dress
of a lady, if not also of a gentleman, till late in the seventeenth
century. Portraits of the beauties of those days, preserved
for us in the engravings of Wierx, Goltzius, de Gheyn,
Kilian, Hollar, Abraham Bosse and many others, almost

GEM OF THE ORDER OF THE
GOLDEN FLEECE, WITH A BLUE
DIAMOND AND A LARGE RUBY

*Made by Jacquelin after a
drawing by Gay. Worn by
Louis XV*

invariably show a mirror, squar
octagonal or round, in settings of tl
most varied materials, sometimes as tl
centre-piece of a fan, but more ofte
attached to the girdle by a ribbon
a chain. The former Rosey collectic
in Dresden contained many seventeentl
century specimens in tiny frames
tortoiseshell, ivory, silver-gilt, steel (
shagreen, decorated with miniature
etchings or little reliefs in silver foi
The mirror as an article of person;
adornment disappeared from the tin
that the wall-mirror, giving large
better and clearer reflections, began t
take shape. But this did not occ
till the second half of the seventeent
century. It was in 1688 that a Frenc
craftsman discovered a method (
casting glass for mirrors, which hithert
had had to be blown. This began
new era for the mirror; it cease
to be a personal ornament, but a
tained value which has steadily increased as a decoration f
the dwelling-room. The pocket-mirror, no longer flaunte

became a purely utilitarian
toilet accessory. Even so
it aroused the ire of the
moralists. "Many women
actually have mirrors in their
snuff-boxes," writes Abraham a S. Clara, "so that
they may flatter the eye at
the same time as the nose!"

An ornament resembling
the pocket-mirror, and carried like it round the neck

206

BROOCH IN PEARLS AND PRECIOUS STON
WHICH BELONGED TO ANNE OF AUSTR
QUEEN OF FRANCE

r at the girdle, was the scent-box, called in France pomme de senteur" because it was usually made round, n the shape of a ball or an apple. The Middle Ages loved trong scents, believing them to be wholesome and a pro- ection against infectious disease; the stronger the odour the reater the virtue attributed to it. Musk was in highest

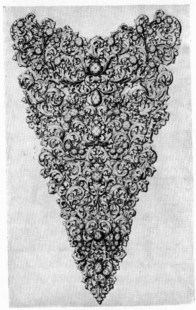

Design by J. B. Grondoni   Brussels, 1715

ORNAMENT WITH DIAMONDS

favour, so much so that "musk-ball" became a common term for the scent-box, even when the perfume contained was not musk. Ambergris was esteemed next to musk, not merely on account of its pleasant smell but also as an aphrodisiac and medicine. Besides these myrrh, incense, iris, and violet were used and in the course of time perfumes became extraordinarily numerous. In 1628 Philip Hainhofer put perfumes of Egyptian and Indian balms and sweet-scented essences of roses, cloves,

LARGE DIAMOND BROOCH IN THE FORM OF A BOW

cinnamon, citron, rosemary, marjoram and anise into a writing-table intended for the Grand Duke of Tuscany. All these ingredients were often mixed together to form a single ball about the size of a walnut. Oliver de la Haye, who in 1348 wrote a poem describing the Black Death, mentions these "artificial apples, made of ambergris and many other noble substances, which smell very strong, refresh the brain and give protection against foul airs."

They were enclosed in filigree holders of precious metals, decorated with enamels and set with precious stones, and they were worn as ornaments, very frequently, for example, as pendants to a rosary. The earliest specimens now remaining are probably the golden apples filled with musk, which ambassadors

NECKLACE OF QUEEN MARIA LECZINSKA

With "le Régent" (a large diamond of the French Crown) in the centre

208

PLATE XIV

FUR COLLAR OF DUCHESS ANNA OF BAVARIA

After the Miniature by Hans Mielich, circa 1550
National Museum, Munich

Designs by Mondon *Paris, c.* 1740
EARRINGS AND TRINKETS IN DIAMONDS

f King Baldwin of Jerusalem presented to the Emperor in
174. The next are heard of in French inventories about
380. King Charles V possessed great numbers of "pommes
e senteur," each more costly than the last, set with rubies,
meralds, garnets and Scottish pearls; most precious of all
vas one of amber set in gold with eight small and two larger
•earls, attached to a sky-blue ribbon which ended in a single
reat pearl. About the same date, Louis I, Duke of Anjou,
•wned a "pomme de senteur" of amber, set in gold enamel,
•n a rosary of real pearls, and also a "noisette de senteur"
•f gold with the inscription "Ave Maria, gratia plena, Dominus
ecum." In 1400 the King of France bought a golden "pomme
le senteur" filled with musk, in a setting of pearls and diamonds.
`he Duc de Berry must have been particularly fond of these
oys, for he had a musk-apple on a slender chain, made to
•pen and show a portrait (painted in 1408) of Jehan d'Orléans,
nd in addition a large "noisette de senteur" of ambergris
nd musk enclosed in gold, and a third in gold set with sapphires

P   209

and pearls. This last may be the actual specimen which tl
Duke of Bedford took from the French crown jewels in 142
In 1484 the Archduke Siegmund of Austria bought twent
seven musk-apples, in a single transaction, from the mercha
Adrian Stabler.

"Musk-apples" were not uniformly round in shape. Cha
lotte d'Albert, Duchess of Valentinois, the widow of Cesa
Borgia, at her death in 1514, left some enclosed in gold filigr
in the shape of pomegranates. The Emperor Charles
possessed similar ones, and also one that was heart-shaped i
gold enamel. In 1528 the Archduchess Anne of Austria becan
possessed of a gold "musk-apple in the shape of an Agnus Dei
and on her death in 1547 she left a gold musk-apple wit
a miniature of herself and her husband. This great lady al
owned a Parisian girdle with two hundred and sixty-eigl
studs, "ending in a large enamelled musk-apple," and a rosar
of agate-stones with a silver-gilt musk-apple. Musk-appl
long survived in the form of pendants to the rosary, an
Hieronymus Tucher of Nuremberg bought himself a rosar
of jet with a silver-gilt musk-apple. As late as 1706 Fath
Leo Wolff of Vienna describes the custom of attaching litt
silver skulls, filled with balsams, to rosaries.

None the less, in the course of the sixteenth century, tl
use of the musk-apple began to wane, not because the nee
for strong perfumes was past, but, on the contrary, becau
this particular contrivance was found inadequate. The wel
known collector and traveller, Philip Hainhofer, boasts th
at the Bavarian court in 1611 he was noted for always smellin
strongly of roses. Admiration seems to have gone to h
head, and, not content to leave well alone, he tells us himse
that on one occasion he so drenched himself in civet, ambergr
and musk that he became speechless and almost fainted.

In France the last "pommes de senteur" were made f
King Francis I, and though such articles are to be found i
inventories of the possessions of the German and Austria
Habsburgs a few decades later they may be safely regarded a
simply heirlooms; possibly they were those very musk-appl

Maria   *Paris, c.* 1765

DESIGNS

Below :
EARRING IN DIAMONDS
BELONGING TO QUEEN
MARIE ANTOINETTE

Right and Left: CHATELAINE IN SILVER
German work of the Eighteenth Century. (*National Museum, Munich*)

Designs by Erasmus Hornig   *Nuremburg, 1562*

Two Étuis for Needles and Thimbles

which the daughter of Charles the Bold brought in her dowry
Again, a collection of musk-apples in gold, shaped like pome
granates, pine-cones, pears and hearts, was among the valuable
pledged to Queen Elizabeth in 1578 by the reigning house o
the Netherlands at Antwerp. Items of such are given in inventories of the legacies of Queen Catherine of Poland in 1570
the Emperor Maximilian II in 1578, the Archduke Charle
of Steiermark in 1590, and, finally, in that of the Archduke
Charles, Grand Master of the Teutonic Order, who died ir
1626, and whose property included a gold musk-apple set with
a pointed diamond, ten turquoises and ten rubies, valued a
sixty reichstalers. In 1619 the Imperial Treasury at Vienna
still contained "a filigree musk-apple in pure gold, surrounding

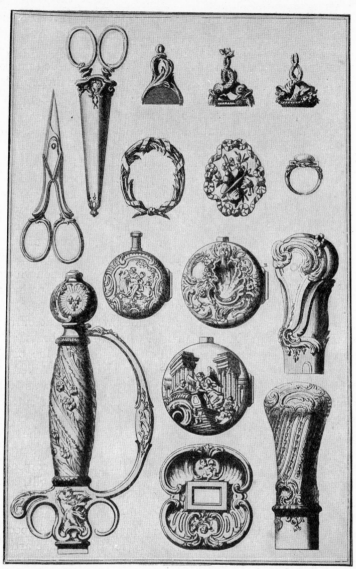

Designs by Lucotte　　　　　　　　　　　　　　*Paris, c.* 1770

SCISSORS, TRINKETS, WATCHES, SWORD-HILT, AND WALKING-STICK HANDLES

a blue silk ball for use in times of infection." In 1608, at the trial of Philip Lang, ex-chamberlain and fallen favourite of the Emperor Rudolph II, one of the chief charges brought against him was that he had embezzled "five enamelled musk-apples." Thereafter the musk-apple vanishes from inventories, superseded by the use of essences, sweet-smelling waters and pomades requiring containers of a different kind.

The exemplary moderation of the Greeks in the use of precious stones as ornaments found no parallel in the Middle Ages, when men and women decked themselves with all the gems they could lay hands on. From early medieval times not only diamonds, but also amethysts, chalcedony, garnets, jacinths, opals, rubies, sapphires, emeralds and topazes were freely used, but no advance had been made in the stone-cutter's art, and the gems must have failed of much of their effect. It was not till the thirteenth century that the polished but uncut gem gave place to the table-cut stone, a fashion which, even so, destroys the life of the stone, giving its colour, perhaps, some chance, but depriving it of all fire.

The demand for jewelry was so widespread that it outran the supply of the genuine article. Accordingly brass and copper were used instead of gold, and paste took the place of precious stones. The Italians were particularly skilled in making imitation gems; so early a writer as Pliny was well acquainted with the art. A special guild of stone-cutters existed in Paris from 1290, and about half a century later, in 1355 and 1365, strict edicts were necessary to forbid the sale of faked jewelry. Even monarchs wore imitation ornaments—in the grave at least—and was it only there? The corpse of the Emperor Frederick II bore a crown of copper gilt, and King Edward I of England, who died in 1307, was buried in seemingly gorgeous apparel of which the "gold" is base metal gilded, while the pearls and precious stones are false. A special study was early made of faking pearls, for the genuine article was very highly prized, even in ancient Rome, and fantastic prices were offered for it. Martial and Seneca, each in his own fashion, satirise the Roman lady's extravagance in pearls.

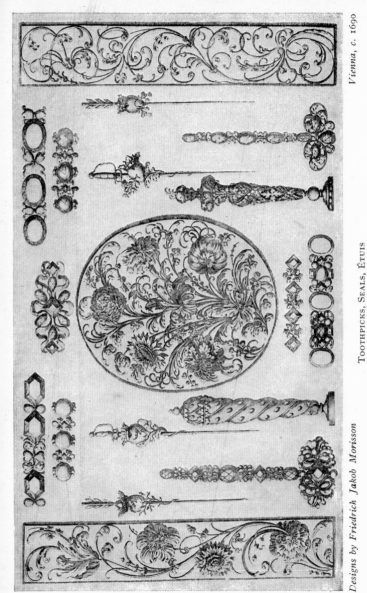

TOOTHPICKS, SEALS, ÉTUIS

Designs by Friedrich Jakob Morisson

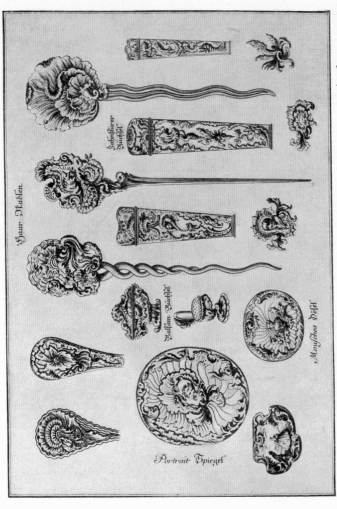

Haar Nadlen.

Schnstürer Büchßt.

Ballan Büchßt.

Mouches Büel.

Portrait Spiegel.

Designs by Johann Martin Engelbrecht

HAIRPINS, SNUFF-BOXES, POCKET-MIRRORS, ETC.

Augsburg, c. 1720

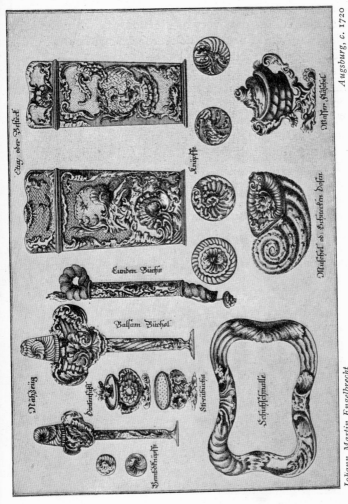

Johann Martin Engelbrecht

DESIGNS

Augsburg, c. 1720

From very early times these were imitated by various method
in pinchbeck and glass, and false pearls made of extremel
thin bronze foil covered with thin clear paste have been du
up in the burial grounds at Reichenhall. Real pearls kep
up in value till the discovery of America, but when the plunde
of the New World flooded the European markets with a glu
of pearls the price fell markedly.

Steadily increasing luxury in the matter of ornaments an
jewelry culminated in the fifteenth and sixteenth centuries
when it attained a level which, at any rate as regards th
sheer quantity of jewelry worn by both sexes, could hardl
be surpassed. Both person and garments were smothered i
it. During the fifteenth century the Burgundian court se
the fashions, and in a generation which went very heavily cla
from head to foot, the superabundance of ornament necessaril
displayed itself on hats and other garments. The Bohemia
traveller, Leo von Rozmital, inspecting the treasures of Phili
the Good, particularly admired the duke's hat, which wa
valued at 60,000 crowns. The hat of Charles the Bold, whicl
formed part of the booty captured by the Swiss at Granson
was adorned with a gold coronet set with large pearls, sapphire
and rubies, and a sixfold pearl cord with a clasp of diamond
pearls and rubies; Jacob Fugger bought it cheap, yet th
price was 4,300 florins. When Duke Philip the Good met th
Emperor Frederick at Besançon in 1442 he wore a scarf se
with pearls and rubies to the value of a hundred thousan
talers, and at a festival in Lille he is said to have carried mor
than a million's worth of jewels on his person.

Under the influence of Burgundian modes, garments wer
lavishly sewn with gold and precious stones, a custom whic
persisted till the beginning of the seventeenth century. I
1411 a goldsmith, Jean Mainfroy, supplied the Burgundia
court with two hundred and twenty hop leaves in silver fo
a green cloth riding suit, seven thousand five hundred silve
rings for a pair of sleeves in black cloth, two thousand silve
leaves for the sleeve of a dress, eleven thousand two hundre
small circular disks, seven hundred and four rings and seve

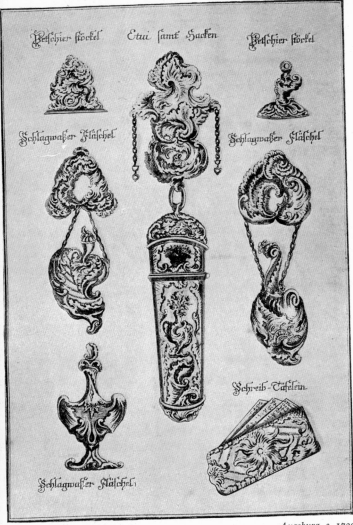

Petschier stöckel   Etui samt Hacken   Petschier stöckel

Schlagwaßer Fläschel   Schlagwaßer Fläschel

Schreib-Täfelein

Schlagwaßer Fläschel

Johann Martin Engelbrecht   *Augsburg, c. 1720*

DESIGNS

219

Design by Johann Jakob Baumgartner   *Augsburg, c.* 1725
SNUFF-BOX LID

hundred imitation flies for a dress and mantle. At her marriag
with Count Richemont in 1423, Princess Margaret of Bu
gundy wore a dress sewn over entirely with little disks of gi
and silvered copper.

The example thus set was zealously followed in all countrie
In the trousseau provided by Pope Alexander VI for his daughte
Lucrezia on her marriage with Duke Alfonso d'Este, each dres
cost from fifteen to twenty thousand ducats, single sleeve
cost as much as three hundred ducats, and the hats, to matc
each costume, averaged ten thousand ducats each. Th
Duchess Beatrice of Milan possessed eighty-four magnificen
gowns in this style, their bodices stitched over with pearl
emeralds and rubies.

This fashion of overloading dress material with preciou
stones and pearls actually increased in the epoch dominate
by Spanish modes. The device of outlining patterns in heav
brocades with real pearls was very much in favour. Th
Electress Elizabeth of Brandenburg, consort of Joachim I
had in her trousseau three pearl-stitched petticoats, valued i
all at six thousand florins. An inventory taken in 1549 of th
possessions of the Archduchess Catherine of Austria mention
twenty-eight gowns heavily stitched in pearls, and Anna, "Quee
of the Romans," was able in 1545 to pledge one of her pearl

Design by Johann Jakob Baumgartner   Augsburg, c. 1725
SNUFF-BOX LID

crusted sleeves for five hundred and fifty ducats.   A private
omeranian lady of noble rank, Frau von Finṫke, possessed
pearl-stitched dress worth fifteen thousand florins.   All this
magnificence, however, can hardly have been becoming; the
wearers of such dresses must have been almost unable to move,
nd it is told of the Pomeranian lady above mentioned that
er gown was so stiff that when at Mass she was unable to
neel down according to custom at the moment of consecration.
Only the influx of American pearls can explain this sudden
avishness in their use.   Queen Anna, wife of the future Emperor
Maximilian II, received 3,384 single pearls in the course of
545.   An inventory, dated 1569, of the goods of the Archduke
Ferdinand of the Tyrol, counts his pearls up to six thousand
nd reckons the rest by weight.   Queen Catherine of Poland,
n Austrian archduchess by birth, left a thousand pearls at
er death.   And so it goes on all though the century.   Mon-
aigne observed on his Italian travels that the ladies' dresses
were entirely covered with pearls and precious stones.   In
594 Gabrielle d'Estrées, Henry IV's mistress, appeared at a
ourt function in a dress of black atlas so loaded with pearls
nd gems that she could not stand without assistance.

The fashions in dress had a great deal to do with this super-
bundance of jewelry.   Ladies and gentlemen alike had their

221

P. Moreau   *Paris, c. 1770*

TWO DESIGNS FOR ÉTUIS

clothes "slashed" to show the lining beneath; these slashing
were then drawn together at intervals and clasped by mean
of small gems, hooks or buttons, with the result that the garmen
appeared studded with ornaments. King Francis I ordered n
fewer than 13,600 gold buttons from his court jeweller for
single black velvet suit. In 1583 Henry III had eightee
dozen large silver buttons made in the shape of death's-head
The Archduke Ernest left at his death more than twenty doze
ornamental buttons, and Queen Catherine of Poland five doze
gold buttons, set with rubies and diamonds and valued at abou
seven hundred pounds in pre-war money. Hans Meinhar
von Schönberg, a private gentlemen, possessed forty-two gol
doublet buttons, each one set with seven diamonds.

Moreover, doublets, sleeves and gowns were sewn with sma
gold disks. Rosette-shaped ornaments were most in favou
but the choice depended on the whim or taste of the individu
wearer of either sex. The Archduke Ferdinand of the Tyrol an
Philipine Welser left among their property about two thousan
gold rosettes, either enamelled or set with pearls, sapphire
rubies and diamonds. In 1557 King Maximilian gave h
sister, the Queen of Poland, a hundred gold rosettes, eac
adorned with three serpents in enamel. The Archduke Erne
left two hundred and ninety-two gold rosettes. Cardin
Albert of Mainz possessed little clasps in gold and gem
shaped like birds, stags, eagles, etc., as ornaments for h
secular garments; they are valued, in the inventory taken c
his death, at from fifty-four to five hundred and fifty flori
apiece. Philipine Welser possessed a vast number of suc
articles, a hundred and forty-one gold tortoises set with tu
quoises, thirty gold frogs, a hundred and thirty-six gold lizard
forty-seven gold "S's," nine hundred and fifty-six roun
garnets in gold settings, etc. The demand for precious ston
for apparel was so insistent that on one occasion King Philip
of Spain sent his third wife, Isabella of Valois, a huge dish
"salad," in which emeralds represented the green leaves, topaz
the oil, rubies the vinegar, and pearls and diamonds the sa

All this dress ornament, however, by no means exclud
personal jewelry. Both ladies and gentlemen wore earring
chains, finger-rings and bracelets, and Luther once spoke
woman as "a ravening beast, never sated with ornament
Rings, pendants and medallions for the hat predominate
Rings were worn not only on every finger, but on every joi
of every finger, even on the thumb. In portraits of the da
hands showing as many as eighteen rings can sometimes l
observed. As if this were not enough, the Margrave Christoph
of Baden strung rings upon the golden chain that adorned l
cap. Princess Anna of Prussia, who was married in 159
had in her trousseau more than a hundred rings set with rubi
and other precious stones.

The pendant, however, was the most important piece

GOLD SNUFF-BOX.   *Design by*
Lalonde, Paris, c. 1780

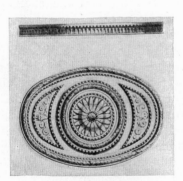

GOLD SNUFF-BOX.   *Design by*
Lalonde, Paris, c. 1780

DESIGN FOR A
FLASK (*Lalonde,*
Paris, c. 1780)

ÉTUI IN
GOLD AND
ENAMEL

Q

Design by P. Moreau GOLD SNUFF-BOX *Paris,* 1771

Renaissance jewelry; upon this the resources of technique and fancy were expended to the utmost. Its construction is quite free and independent of the medallion. In form it is architectonic, devised to show single figures or scenes in high relief, the subjects being very frequently borrowed from classic mythology. The fount of invention seems inexhaustible and overflows in a superabundance of designs which come easily and naturally from the artist's hand. The watchword colour; brightly-coloured enamel and gems predominate, killing the effect of the gold, and artistry of arrangement and conception is valued more than the sheer worth of the gems employed.

Gems continued to take a secondary place for the reason that even towards the end of the fifteenth century the method of cutting was defective and failed to bring out their full effect. In 1456 Ludwig van Berquen of Bruges discovered the art of polishing the diamond with its own powder. Charles the Bold placed his valuable diamonds in this man's hands and paid him three thousand ducats for polishing these famous gems. But facet-cut still remained primitive enough, and even the lozenge cut, which had been used in the case of diamonds since 1520 was a stage in the development of the craft which left much to be desired. The use of foil was still indispensable in the setting of coloured gems, and readers of Benvenuto Cellini's autobiography will remember that he attaches importance to the choice of a suitable backing.

226

Design by P. Moreau   GOLD SNUFF-BOX   *Paris,* 1771

Pendants quivered with hanging pearls, baroque pearls being
y no means despised for this purpose.   On the technical side
1e jeweller's art was enriched by the art of inlay, which was
1uch practised, especially by the Moors.   These pendants
·ere worn without stint by both men and women.   Lucas
·ranach painted portraits of young women with six different
·endants adorning their bare necks, while three more hang on
·ng chains.   Men fastened them in their hats or caps, more
·articularly those magnificent portrait-medallions which the
·talian painters of the day produced in rare perfection.   Hans
Iülich, who from 1552 to 1553 was engaged in painting in
1iniature the jewels of Duchess Anne of Bavaria, (an Austrian
·rchduchess by birth) depicts more pendants than any other
·rt of ornament in what is probably the most artistic inventory
1 existence.

Artists of the first rank co-operated also to make the
·weller's craft one of importance.   Italian goldsmiths of the
·enaissance such as Ghiberti, Cellini, Caradosso and others,
1d German masters such as Dürer, Holbein, Aldegrever,
·rosamer, Virgil Solis, Jamnitzer, de Bry, etc., must not be
·rgotten in this connection; the designs of these latter for
·ieces of jewelry, pendants in particular, stand unrivalled for
·elicacy and taste, are distinguished by a feeling for their

227

medium, and, in the sixteenth century, assured a world-market
for the products of south German workshops.

The excess of personal ornament then common was largely
due to the fact that the dowries of women of means were often
paid in articles of jewelry and precious stones instead of in cash.
Such articles represented savings which could be turned into
money by pawn or sale as occasion arose. In 1440 Queen Elizabeth, widow of Albert II, pledged her jewels for 2,500 gold
gulden, which at that time had the purchasing power of about

EIGHTEENTH-CENTURY SNUFF-BOXES
The Empress Frederick's Collection

fifty gold marks; among them were necklaces and bracelets,
pendants and clasps in gold enamel, set with pearls and rubies.
In 1526 the Electress Elizabeth of Brandenburg pledged her
bridal jewelry to her brother King Christian of Denmark,
with the result that it was lost for ever to herself and her heirs.
The Emperor Charles V, when in need of money for war, asked
his sister, the dowager Queen of Portugal, to pledge her jewelry
for him and also demanded from Margrave John of Brandenburg, then Governor of Valencia, the loan of his personal
ornaments and those of his wife; whether he liked it or not
the Margrave was forced to surrender twelve articles of jewelry
to the value of over 24,000 ducats. Count Christopher of
Oldenburg, having made himself master of Denmark, called
upon the Danish nobility at a Diet in Copenhagen in 1534
to surrender all their womenfolk's jewels—a demand which
cost him the Danish crown. In 1581 Hans von Schweinichen
proposed to celebrate his wedding with great festivities at
Liegnitz, but none of his friends would come, his enemies having

228

Graff   1766

JOHANNA ERDMUTHE, COUNTESS BÜNAU, *née* COUNTESS
SCHÖNFELD, HOLDING A SHUTTLE

spread a rumour that Duke Henry, who was chronically in
money difficulties, intended to use the occasion to relieve the
ladies of all their jewelry!

If one may trust the pictures of Lucas Cranach, de Bruyn
and others, ladies wore heavy gold chains, often wound threefold or fourfold about their necks. The bride estimated the
bridegroom's affection by the weight of the gold chain which
he gave her at the wedding. In 1518 Lucas Rem of Augsburg
presented his betrothed with a gold chain worth ninety-eight
florins, and in 1577 Joachim Brandis of Hildesheim gave Anna

Kleineberg two gold chains, one costing twenty-seven and the other sixty-six gold gulden; in 1587, when he married again, his second wife received one chain worth forty-five florins and another one hundred and five florins. In 1589 Duke Frederick of Liegnitz gave his bride a gold chain worth three hundred Hungarian gulden. Men often wore luck-pennies and portrait-medallions bestowed by princes attached to their gold chains.

In the sixteenth century watches came into use. Peter Henlein, who set up as a locksmith in Nuremberg in 1509, is generally regarded as their inventor. Johannes Cockläus, writing in 1511, tells us that Henlein "makes little clocks in iron with many wheels which can be wound up at will, have no pendulum, go for forty hours, and strike and can be carried in the bosom or in the purse." Henlein, however, was not the inventor of the watch, for before his time portable mechanical time-pieces with horizontal dials were already in existence. These table-watches with spring barrels were the immediate predecessors of the watch proper, and by 1510 they were made small enough to be carried about in a purse. Henlein's service was to make them so minute that they might be attached by a hook to the dress or hung about the neck. His watches, of which no existing specimen can be identified with certainty, were cylindrical in shape with iron works and bronze cases. These early watches were made by locksmiths and compass-makers, though during Henlein's lifetime (he died at Nuremberg in 1540) watch-making became a separate

230

trade. Till about 1540 watches were shaped like pill-boxes, but after Henlein's death the egg-like form described by Rabelais in *Pantagruel* began to appear.

On the technical side the evolution of the watch was very slow; the minute hand did not come for another century, the earlier watches had only an hour hand. Brass, however, soon replaced iron, which was too liable to rust, and after 1590 chain was used instead of catgut on the barrel turned by the spring. None the less, the sixteenth-century watch could chime, and about 1600, could give an alarum. A transparent face for the dial was made of crystal. For the first decade after its invention the watch must have been a rarity. It is true that Holbein painted one in his portrait of Gyszae, a Danzig merchant, as early as 1532, but in April 1547 we find Luther writing to the Abbot Pistorius of Nuremberg to thank him for the gift of a watch as follows: "Through your most welcome gift I feel constrained to become a pupil of our mathematicians in order to learn all the rules and laws of this watch, unique of its kind, for I have never hitherto seen or examined anything similar."

The watch was usually worn on a gold chain about the neck, as may be seen, for example, in portraits of Henry VIII, and accordingly it became frequently a most ornate piece of jewelry. Philipine Welser possessed, as the gift of the Duke of Ferrara, a gold watch enamelled in white, black and blue, set with diamonds, rubies and pearls, with a gold enamelled pouch also adorned with diamonds, rubies and pearls. This fine

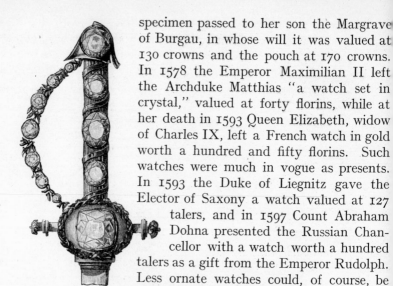

SWORD-HILT OF NAPOLEON
AS FIRST CONSUL, WITH
"LE RÉGENT"

specimen passed to her son the Margrave of Burgau, in whose will it was valued at 130 crowns and the pouch at 170 crowns. In 1578 the Emperor Maximilian II left the Archduke Matthias "a watch set in crystal," valued at forty florins, while at her death in 1593 Queen Elizabeth, widow of Charles IX, left a French watch in gold worth a hundred and fifty florins. Such watches were much in vogue as presents. In 1593 the Duke of Liegnitz gave the Elector of Saxony a watch valued at 127 talers, and in 1597 Count Abraham Dohna presented the Russian Chancellor with a watch worth a hundred talers as a gift from the Emperor Rudolph. Less ornate watches could, of course, be had at a cheaper rate. In 1548 Count Wolrad von Waldeck bought a watch in a gilded case at Augsburg for eighteen talers and a lady's watch for a mere fifteen gulden.

Fashion soon took charge of this attractive invention. Paul von Stetten tells us that in 1558 the young elegants of Augsburg carried small spherical watches which chimed, and in England too we learn that the wearing of a watch was fashionable in the days of Queen Elizabeth. A speech of Malvolio's in *Twelfth Night* shows that the winding of the watch in the presence of others might be a pleasant little gesture of polite swagger. In 1575 a gilded watch was the seventh prize in a shooting contest for the burghers of Vienna.

In the sixteenth century there arose a vogue for very tiny watches. The Emperor Charles V possessed an earring containing a watch with chimes, and watches were not infrequently set in rings. An inventory (taken in 1619) of the Imperial Treasury, Vienna, mentions a great number of watches, among them many set in rings and made to strike. One such specimen exists in the Court Museum, Vienna; it con-

ists of a gold ring with translucent enamelling, set with diamonds and a single emerald, cut with the imperial double-headed
agle, surmounting a watch with an enamelled dial. In 1619,
George Hipp, a Kempten watchmaker, sent the Archduke
Leopold at Innsbruck a model in lead of a watch in a ring,
stimated to cost 100 gulden if executed in gold and enamelling,
r 150 gulden with the addition of chimes. A ring of this

ORNAMENTAL CHAIN IN IRON
Berlin Iron-Foundry

kind made by Jacob Widmann of Augsburg for the Duchess
of Mantua is now in the Morgan collection. As late as the
nineteenth century King Anthony of Saxony wore an eight-
day watch in a ring. During a great part of the seventeenth
century, however, the watch was carried concealed in the
pocket. Until the Thirty Years War the watchmakers of
Germany had a certain renown and Philip Hainhofer mentions
Hipp of Kempten, Sayler of Ulm, Stahel, Boschmann and
Kreutzerer of Augsburg as among the best watchmakers known
to him, but about that time the products of other countries

233

came more to the fore. "If you want trouble, marry a wife buy a watch, or beat a parson," said the Elector Maximilia I of Bavaria, a remark which says little for the quality of th watches of his day.

Such advances as were made in technique at this tim originated in England, or at any rate went to improve the in dustry there. In 1715 "Amaranthes" writes, "English watche are generally held to be the most accurate and the best." Th cause of this was the invention of the spiral spring with a balanc which had been generally adopted by 1690 and which mad the use of a minute hand possible. In the seventeenth centur all kinds of queer shapes were popular, and watches were mad oval, spherical, octagonal, dodecahedral, star-shaped, egg shaped, or in the form of books, almonds, walnuts, heraldi lilies, etc. In 1750 there was in the Treasury, Vienna a watch in the form of a skull, made in silver with a jaw-bon which opened and shut. There is a similar exhibit in the Cour Museum, Vienna, consisting of an egg-shaped watch, the cas made of horn, decorated with gold and enamels, and withi this a silver skull which tells the hours by movements of th jaw-bone. In the Ole Olsen collection there is also a watch i the form of a skull, with pictures of the Creation and the Fal

Specimens of so-called "crucifix-watches" and "abbes watches" are to be seen in the Green Vault, Dresden, an in many private collections. The Archduke Charles, Gran Master of the Teutonic Order, who died in 1626, had a tin watch set in the centre of his gold cross of the Orde Watches were placed in powder-horns (there was one suc in the Imperial Treasury in 1731) and in weapons. In 161 the Elector Christian II of Saxony presented to his brothe Duke John George, a rapier and dagger with chiming watche in their hilts; Hainhofer mentions seeing them in 1629 and the are now in the Historical Museum, Dresden. The number c articles with which the watch was combined increased as tim went on. In 1740 Louis XV gave the Queen a snuff-bo with a watch, and when the Margravine Augusta Sibylla o Baden-Baden died in 1776 she left a walking-stick with

234

CROWN DIAMONDS OF THE GUELPH DYNASTY. DIADEM, NECKLACE OF
BRILLIANTS, EARRINGS, COMPRISING SIX THOUSAND DIAMONDS IN ALL
Valued in 1858 at £120,000

watch in the handle which was valued at six hundred florins.
In the course of time watches were combined with other
instruments. In the treasury of the Wittelsbachs at Munich
there is an oval silver watch by Conrad Rerizer of Augsburg,
with five dials showing hours, months, days, planets, etc. The
Bourgeois collection at Cologne contained a quatrefoil-shaped
watch, its case of rock-crystal, the dial showing upon four
faces the hour, the date, the planets and the phases of the
moon. In the Court Museum, Vienna, there is a watch
shaped like a book which contains a compass, a sundial, a
dial-plate for reckoning the phases of the moon, etc.

In royal circles much stress was laid on magnificence and
costliness of setting. The Infanta Isabella Clara Eugenia
sent her sister-in-law, Queen Margaret of Spain, a small watch
covered with diamonds valued in 1611 at five thousand reals.
The Queen on her death left, besides this, another watch in
gold with her own monogram and that of Philip III in diamonds

235

and rubies. In 1660 the Archduke Leopold William left "the crystal watch he always carried about him and had bought for thirty-five ducats" to his chamberlain, Baron von Unverzagt, while his dwarf and his valet each inherited watches valued at about twenty-four reichstalers. The Archduke had paid eighty-two florins for watches in Venetian paste and thirty-eight florins for a watch in a lapis lazuli case. In 1647 the Great Elector of Brandenburg gave his bride, Louisa Henrietta of Orange, a wedding gift of a little watch set with forty-four big diamonds, valued at four hundred florins.

At the end of the seventeenth century and the beginning of the eighteenth came the repeater watch, the reputed invention of the English watchmaker, Daniel Quare, court watchmaker to George I, with whom he stood in high favour; this man was excused from the observance of certain forms and ceremonies for he was a Quaker who would take no oath nor consent to uncover to anyone about the palace. About the middle of the eighteenth century, improvements in technique allowed the introduction of the seconds hand.

In the eighteenth century miniature-work was brought to a degree of perfection which has never been surpassed, and the utmost pains were expended upon outward adornment. All the resources of the artist's skill and the craftsman's dexterity were drawn upon to beautify the case of the watch. As the watch at this time still hung exposed at the belt or girdle, its costly setting did not fail of full effect. Maria Theresa had a watch in an irregular oval case made of a single emerald; it is still to be seen in the Treasury at the Hofburg. Queen Sophia Dorothea of Prussia was very fond of watches and on her death in 1757 left fifty-one in cases of jasper, lapis lazuli, onyx, cornelian, chrysoprase, etc., all richly adorned with brilliants; the most costly was valued at five hundred talers. Her son, on his death in 1786, left few watches but all were set either with brilliants or coloured gems. Watches were much in vogue as presents and tokens of favour. At a great entertainment given for the ladies at the electoral court of Bavaria on 14 May, 1727, the first prize was a basket of lettuce

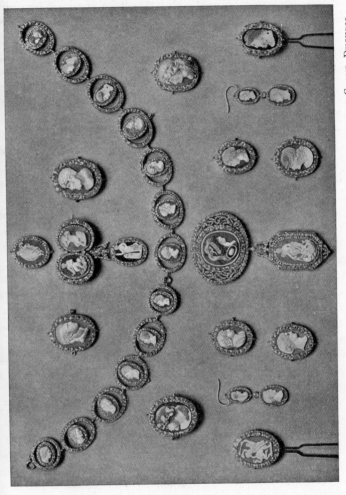

A SET OF CAMEO ORNAMENTS, SET IN DIAMONDS, ONCE THE PROPERTY OF THE GRAND DUCHESS
MARIA PAVLOVNA OF SAXE-WEIMAR AND HER DAUGHTER THE EMPRESS AUGUSTA

Hohenzollern heirlooms

237

concealing a gold repeater watch. The *corbeilles* of French princesses always contained numbers of watches, varying from 650 to 2,400 francs in value. They were mainly intended for presentation to inferiors, and when the Archduchess Maria Amelia married the Duke of Parma in 1769 she took with her to Parma "fine enamelled gold repeater watches with enamelled clasps" for distribution to her waiting women. Frederick the Great of Prussia paid the merchant Gotzkowsky and the jeweller Jordan sums varying from eight to thirteen hundred talers for ladies' watches to be given as presents. These were large sums under Frederick's régime but they dwindle by comparison with expenditure for similar purposes incurred at the French court. In 1773 the Comtesse d'Artois received a watch costing 6,000 francs, the key and signet costing 1,200 francs and the accompanying chatelaine 16,350 francs. Another watch set with brilliants, emeralds and rubies cost 19,000 francs. At a time when the vogue for buttons on men's coats reached its zenith the Comte d'Artois the future Charles X, wore watches as buttons.

The ownership of a watch must long have remained rare among the German middle classes. Johann Heinrich Voss received his first watch as a present from the Syndic when he was already headmaster at Eutin, and Johann Salomo Semler became a university professor before he owned one. When the Austrians took Vilshofen in 1745 one of their non-commissioned officers looted a watch from a lieutenant in the captured town but was obliged at the same time to ask the owner to wind it up for him as he had no idea how to set about it. As long as the watch was worn outside the pocket its shape remained unwieldy and thick, but when, at the close of the eighteenth century it began to be carried in the pocket it became flat and slim in build. At the same time it ceased to be an article of personal adornment, so that the case became plain and simple and in the nineteenth century meaningless guilloche pattern ousted all other manifestations of the goldsmith's craft in regard to the watch; from then on it ceased to be a work of art and became a mere industrial mass-product.

JEWELRY OF THE DUCHESS OF DEVONSHIRE. ANTIQUE CAMEOS SET IN
GOLD WITH ENAMELS AND DIAMONDS (*Hancock, London*, 1857, *and valued
at that time at £20,000. Worn by Countess Granville at the Coronation of
the Czar Alexander II of Russia in Moscow*)

Under the heading of sixteenth-century dress-ornament mu
be mentioned the fur collar (called in Germany the "Flohpel
chen" or flea-fur because it was believed to attract tho
noxious insects). Skins in the shape of sable, marten, polec
and weasel, were stuffed and supplied with heads and claws
all kinds of precious materials. In the portraits of Italia
ladies dating after the middle of the century these little article
of attire may often be seen carried in the sitter's hand. Suc
fur collars are mentioned in an inventory of the goods of th
Duke of Burgundy in 1467 and other isolated examples belon
to about that date, but a century later they become ver
frequent. The Duke of Ferrara gave his wife a sable fur wit
a head in gold set with twelve rubies, three diamonds, thre
emeralds, and four pearls. At her death in 1572 Quee
Catherine of Poland left a sable fur with a gold head set wit
precious stones and valued at 750 talers. Philipine Wels
left ornaments for a fur collar consisting of the head of a sabl
in gold, set with five rubies and five emeralds, the eyes i
garnets, a pearl in the mouth, and the four paws also in gol
and set with rubies and emeralds. A sable left by the Margra
vine of Burgau, who died in 1580, had a head of solid gold se
with diamonds, rubies and pearls and was valued at 310 crown
the fur itself being estimated at 20 crowns and the cost
making at 30 crowns.

The rosary may also be regarded as an article of adornmer
even though its first use was purely as an aid to devotion
It is said to have originated at an ecclesiastical assembly a
Auxerre in 1095, though the Dominican Order claim that
was invented by their founder, St. Dominic. As it wa
carried visibly, in the hand or at the girdle, the instinct fc
adornment inevitably took account of it, and the most costl
materials came to be considered barely good enough for s
pious a use. In the days of Charles VI French inventorie
mention valuable specimens in solid gold, enamelled, set wit
precious stones, made entirely of real pearls, etc. Ther
were also dozens of rosaries in chalcedony, jet, rock-crysta
amber, mother-of-pearl, agate, cornelian, amethyst, cora

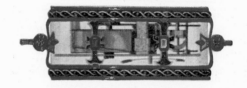

PLATE XV

SIXTEENTH CENTURY WATCHES

NECKLACE OF OPALS AND DIAMONDS

J. Turner, London ; presented by Queen Victoria of England to her daughter Victoria, the future Empress Frederick, in 1858

onyx, lapis lazuli, etc. A distinction was made between rosaries with only ten beads, and the complete "paternoster" with fifteen times ten beads (the number of the Psalms of David) and fifteen larger beads to mark off the beads by tens. There were also smaller rosaries of sixty-three beads (the number of the years of Our Lady) with seven large ones between, and others with thirty-three beads (the number of the years of Our Lord) with five large ones symbolising the five wounds of the Crucified. Each group of ten small beads (for the same number of Ave Marias) and one large bead (for the paternoster) was called a "decade." The rosary was hung about the neck or at the girdle or was wound about the arm. The Emperor Ferdinand I gave his daughter, Duchess Eleanor of Mantua, a rosary with ninety-six gold beads as a bridal wreath at her marriage in 1561. Among simple folk, no doubt, the rosary was often the only ornament they could call their own, and the wife of one Leonhard Brotlieb, a collector of customs at the Lueg Pass, left at her death seven rosaries in coral and chalcedony with musk-apples for the larger beads.

Among the great and well-to-do the rosary formed another welcome occasion for luxury and display. The Electress Elizabeth of Brandenburg had in her dowry, at her marriage in 1502, a "large paternoster" in gold, the beads set with pearls, rubies, emeralds and diamonds; it was valued at 260 gulden Charlotte d'Albret, Duchess of Valentinois and widow of Cesare Borgia, who died in 1514, had a rosary made of gold enamelled beads hollowed to contain perfumes. An inventory taken in 1528 of the goods of Anna, "Queen of the Romans," lists, among others, one rosary of a hundred and fifty-nine beads in gold and twenty-seven in amethyst. After the Reformation this accessory of devotion continued to exist, of course, only amongst Catholics, who went on producing and using most ornate specimens. In 1561 the Duke of Mantua gave his bride, the Archduchess Eleanor, more than forty rosaries in coral, lapis lazuli, cornelian, agate, rock-crystal, etc, all set in pure gold. At competitions in marksmanship held among the citizens of Vienna in 1575 and 1578 prizes were offered consisting of rosaries in chalcedony, mother-of-pearl, coral etc., in silver settings. King Philip II left a rosary of gold beads, each one set with nine rubies, the crucifix attached containing ten rubies. It was valued at 396 ducats. When the fall of the Emperor Rudolph II's long-established favourite, the chamberlain Philip Lang, was brought about by his enemies in 1608, among the many charges made against him at his trial was that of having embezzled two agate and cornelian rosaries. An inventory taken in 1611 of the property of the deceased Queen Margaret of Spain, consort of Philip III, mentions a rosary in gold and diamonds, containing fifty real pearls, of the value of 1,250 ducats, and another in amber and gold enamelled beads, set with diamonds, valued at 800 ducats. In 1611 Philip Hainhofer visited Johann Conrad von Gemmingen, Bishop of Eichstatt, and admired a gold paternoster, set with diamonds and pearls, in the bishop's possession. A small rosary of only eleven beads left by the Archduke Charles, Grand Master of the Teutonic Order, was valued in the inventory at from seventy to a hundred and twelve talers. It was a splendour-loving generation that saw the sixteenth century out, and men were in no way behind women in the passion for adornment. At the christening of the dauphin, the future Louis XIII, Marshal le Bassompierre wore a suit of cloth-of-gold stitched with real pearls and weighing fifty pounds. The Duke of Buckingham attended the wedding of Charles I in Paris in 1635 wearing a suit stitched all over with diamonds of the estimated value of 500,000 francs. The same nobleman once attended a court function in a short cloak of grey velvet covered with real pearls which were intentionally stitched so loosely that they fell to the floor at every movement; his Grace abandoned them to the finders.

Even apart from these somewhat exceptional cases the gentlemen of those days may be said to have covered themselves with jewelry; chains, earrings, brace-

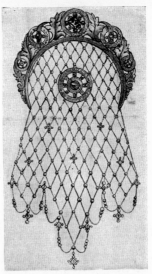

HAIRNET IN PEARLS, DIAMONDS AND EMERALDS (*Presented as a wedding gift by Queen Victoria to her daughter the Princess Victoria, the future Empress Frederick of Germany*)

lets were everyday wear. The great Sully, Henry IV's right-hand man in matters of statecraft, never laid aside his bracelets till his death in 1641, and we may safely picture Shakespeare as wearing earrings and bracelets. King Christian paced his decks wearing the pearl earrings which we wonder at to-day in portraits of that most martial of Denmark's rulers. Hats, too, were richly bejewelled. Endymion Porter while attached to the English embassy in Madrid wore his wife's diamond necklace as a hat-band, and in 1650 the Governor of Virginia commissioned a lady to buy him a hat-band at The Hague for the price of a thousand ducats or so.

The ladies equalled if they did not outvie the men. At the christening of her three eldest children on 14 September, 1606, Maria de' Medici wore a gown stitched with thirty-two thousand pearls and three thousand diamonds. Describing a reception

243

at the Louvre in 1612 the *Mercure de France* remarks that th
gowns of the Queen of Navarre and the Comtesse de Soisson
were so covered with precious stones that it was impossibl
to say of what stuff they were made. Apart from gowns thu
begemmed women covered every available part of the perso
with jewels. In the first decade of the seventeenth centur
an ornament of remarkable size worn upon the breast becam
a notable feature of the lady's toilet; this was a brooch designe
to secure the ends of the lace collar. It may be well to mentio
here, however, that the positively astounding wealth of jewelr
often seen in portraits of this period by no means alway
faithfully represents the property of the persons portrayed, th
painter, by an act of supererogation, often endowing his model
with a wealth they were far from actually possessing. On
remembers how the Vicar of Wakefield's good lady requeste
the painter of her portrait "not to be too frugal of his diamond
in her stomacher and hair." In fact, as opposed to fiction
English ladies who had their portraits painted in 1640 paid te
shillings extra if they wished the artist to put a fine rope of pearl
about their throats. Lady Sussex, on the other hand, writing t
Sir Edmund Verney, complains that Van Dyck has overdone th
diamonds in her portrait and put in far more than she possesse

This excess of ornament persisted while Spain set the fashions
the style of cut and the materials then in favour demande
a wealth of ornament to set them off, but when the garment
of both sexes became lighter and artificial paddings an
stiffenings went out there was no longer either room or occasio
for so much jewelry. Accordingly, from about the middle o
the seventeenth century onwards, ornament steadily decline
in quantity and, in the case of men, almost entirely disappeare
Technical changes contributed largely to this result. In th
mid-seventeenth century Dutch lapidaries discovered th
advantages of brilliant-cut stones—that is to say that th
facets of a diamond must be cut in multiples of eight if th
stone is to reveal all its inherent beauty. They began wit
sixteen facets and went on to thirty-two, but the proces
was difficult and many excellent diamonds were still prism

244

Necklace of One Hundred and Eighteen Pearls and Two Thousand
Diamonds as a Chain for the so-called "Dagmar Cross" of A.D. 1212
(*The work of Julius Didrichsen, Copenhagen, 1863, and presented by the King
of Denmark to his daughter, the Princess of Wales. Valued then at £7000*)

cut, table - cut or rose - cut. It was about this time that Hortensio Borgio of Venice spoiled the Koh-i-noor, making it look like a piece of rock-crystal by unskilful cutting, and it was not till 1852 that Coster re-cut this famous stone, spending thirty-eight days in the process and reducing its weight from a hundred and eighty-six to a hundred and six carats; it gained, however, in beauty what it lost in weight. In 1652 Cardinal Mazarin had the twelve biggest diamonds in the French regalia cut as brilliants.

This new method of cutting radically altered the fashion in jewelry. Ornaments hitherto had been small works of art upon the production of which imagination and technical skill had been lavished, but now the goldsmith and the jeweller parted company; the precious stone itself became the centre of interest, and has remained so to this day. Settings of later date than the mid-seventeenth century have no role of their own to play, being mere framework for displaying the gems. For this reason diamonds were very often set in silver, stones were crowded together, and the simplest and flattest designs were chosen, such as bows, rosettes and disks, since they displayed the diamonds to greatest advantage.

Buttons became about this time the only form of jewelry permissible for gentlemen. Louis XIV, of course, set the mode and on special occasions, such as receptions of foreign ambassadors, wore as much as twelve to fifteen million francs worth of diamonds. "He sank under the weight of them," writes Saint-Simon. Even before 1684 that monarch possessed a hundred and four buttons, each made of a single diamond and in that year he had a diamond of fifty-two carats split in two to make a pair of buttons. In 1686 the court jeweller delivered him a set of ornaments for a waistcoat consisting of forty-eight studs and ninety-six edgings for the corresponding button - holes, comprising in all eight hundred and sixteen coloured gems and one thousand eight hundred and twenty four diamonds to the value of 360,000 francs. In the following year Louis paid 377,500 francs for a set of twenty-one coat buttons, each made of a single diamond.

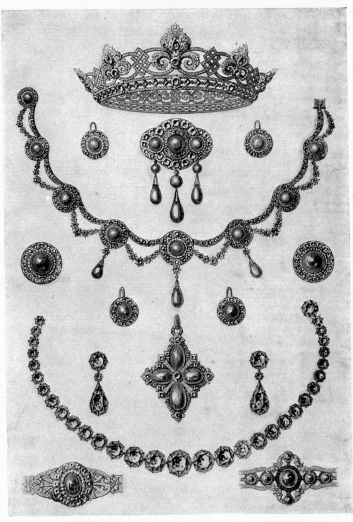

ORNAMENTS IN DIAMONDS AND PEARLS FORMING WEDDING PRESENTS FROM
ENGLISH CITIES TO THE PRINCESS OF WALES IN 1863

The other European rulers did their best to live up to this example. In 1665, at his wedding with the Infanta Margaret, the Emperor Leopold wore a suit of cloth-of-gold having large diamonds for buttons. The Elector Maximilian Emmanuel of Bavaria bought a set of diamond and ruby buttons in Brussels for which he paid 274,800 florins. Among the Saxon crown jewels in the Green Vault at Dresden are sets of buttons made for Augustus the Strong, including rubies, sapphires, emeralds and topazes, thirty waistcoat and thirty coat buttons of rose-cut diamonds, and the same number in brilliants. Frederick, first King of Prussia, possessed while still Elector eight dozen diamond buttons, each consisting of a large central diamond surrounded by six smaller diamonds; these had been set at The Hague and were worth 5,000 talers in all. In addition Frederick had five dozen diamond buttons worth 200 talers apiece. At his coronation on 18 January, 1701 he wore a scarlet coat stitched in gold and adorned with large diamond buttons, each worth 3000 talers. When Louis XIV was barely six years old a little waistcoat was made for him with thirty-six ruby buttons. In the Habsburg regalia in Vienna in 1731 were a set of thirty-five buttons for a Spanish court-dress, each one consisting of a single large brilliant, and other sets of buttons by the dozen made of brilliants set with sapphires, turquoises, rubies and topazes for coats and waistcoats.

Buttons for ladies' dresses were no less costly than those worn by men. In 1698 Mlle d'Aubigné, a niece of Mme de Maintenon, received a set of sixteen sleeve buttons valued at 12,000 francs, as a wedding gift from Louis XIV, and when the Regent's daughter married the Duke of Modena in 1723 she was presented with twelve buttons, each made of a single coloured gem and seven brilliants, and worth in all 35,000 francs. In 1765 the Infanta Maria Louisa married the future Charles IV of Spain and received from an aunt as a wedding present six buttons, comprising a hundred and nineteen brilliants to the value of 45,000 francs. As all were not able to afford real stones for those personal ornaments in which

248

BRACELET OF QUEEN MARIA OF NAPLES, PRESENTED BY THE LADIES
OF BORDEAUX (*made by Froment Meurice, Paris*)

the mode required their presence, imitations were substituted.
In 1758 the jeweller Strass discovered the form of imitation
which bears his name to this day, and his very effective stones
were in great demand.

On the whole, however, remarkably little ornament was worn
in the eighteenth century. It may have been that the cost
of wearing jewels became almost prohibitive after the great
financial catastrophe precipitated in France by the operations of
John Law, and, what was really a matter of domestic economy
in France in the ordinary course of things, set the fashion
abroad. However that may be, portraits of ladies, during
the rococo period show the sitters strikingly *décolletées*, yet
in most cases without jewelry round their necks. About the
middle of the century, however, earrings of extravagant length
called "girandoles" came in and hung almost to the wearers'
shoulders.

To compensate for the restraints laid upon them by fashion
in the matter of personal ornament, both ladies and gentlemen began to carry a number of small articles in their pockets
made of materials so costly and so richly bejewelled that they
may fairly count, perhaps, as personal adornments. Under
this heading come such articles as netting-needles and toothpicks, but mainly the numerous kinds of small boxes from
which both sexes appear to have been inseparable throughout
the century. Their uses were almost as varied as the materials
of which they were made, though no substance was thought too
costly or too rare to be made into a box. Many of the uses

to which these little boxes were put, such as holding sweets, comfits and perfumes, were long established, but contents of other kinds, snuff, beauty-patches and cosmetics, came in with the rococo period. The main point of interest, however, is that no other age expended such art and skill upon these tiny receptacles or endowed them with such exquisite form. A survey of the subject almost tempts one to speak of a special "art of box-making," so great was the cost, so perfect the technique and so varied the invention expended at that time upon these tiny products of fancy and luxury.

As regards material, we find gold, silver, copper, brass, bronze, ivory, mother-of-pearl, tortoiseshell, ebony and all kinds of stones, such as Florence marble, malachite, lapis lazuli, blood-jasper, agate, chalcedony, cornelian, lava and rock-crystal, besides artificial substances such as papier mâché, burgau, mosaic, enamel, lacquer, porcelain and paste. Use was even made of crabs' claws, rhinoceros-horn and prepared shark-skin, called in France after the inventor of the process, "galuchat." These substances were turned, embossed, chased and engine-turned and often lavishly set with diamonds and other precious stones.

During the eighteenth century these little boxes were the characteristic ornaments of good society. It was always *bon ton* to carry several upon the person; the correct air with which to take them out of the pocket and play with them was an item in the polite education of both sexes. They were the most popular of all objects as presents, the courts of Europe lavishly setting the example in this matter. In the nineteenth century those in authority were able to get off lightly with some trumpery tin decoration and a yard or so of ribbon, but in the seventeenth and eighteenth centuries, before the evolution of the civil-list, they were forced to make deep inroads on the common purse and give objects of real value to those who had rendered, or were expected to render, faithful service.

The French court under Louis XIV instituted this very costly convention, leaving lesser princes no choice but to follow their admired model as far as their leaner purses would allow. In the case of Germany, this had at least the advantage of giving an effective impetus to the development of the native goldsmith's craft, whose products soon reached a level of per-

CENTRE-PIECE OF A GIRDLE BELONGING TO THE EMPRESS EUGÉNIE
Made by Bapst, Paris, 1867

fection unsurpassed even by those of Paris. Legislation gave vigorous assistance. On 16 November, 1740, Frederick the Great forbade the import of French articles of "bijouterie" in the precious metals, with the result that Berlin manufacturers, as Sarre has pointed out, soon supplied all Germany with gold boxes, étuis, scent-bottles, etc., such as had hitherto been

"GRECIAN" DIADEM OF THE EMPRESS EUGÉNIE, WITH
SIX HUNDRED AND TWELVE DIAMONDS
Made by Bapst, Paris, 1867

imported at great cost from Paris. Theremin, a Berlin jeweller who had been apprenticed four and a half years in London and three and a half years in Paris, was especially renowned both for taste and good workmanship. Gotzkowsky attracted the most highly skilled workers in gold, enamellers, jewellers and engravers to the Prussian capital, while the brothers Jordan, the Reclams and the Ermans won wide repute. Dresden did not lag behind Berlin and, between 1720 and 1770, produced many notable examples of the goldsmith's craft, the names of such Saxon jewellers as Taddel, Hofmann and Neuber becoming famous throughout Germany.

At court small and very ornate boxes formed the principal tokens of esteem exchanged between persons of rank, or, on occasion, bestowed on their inferiors. A gold box, was frequently, in effect, a disguised money payment, sometimes rendered more graceful by the fact that the portrait of the donor in enamel or miniature painting adorned the lid.[1]

The seal was frequently set upon royal betrothals by the mutual presentation of boxes. In 1679 Charles III of Spain gave his unfortunate bride a gold box set with diamonds worth 200,000 talers, about one and a half million francs in pre-war

---

[1] The author has treated of this custom very fully in his *Miniatures and Silhouettes* (J. M. Dent & Sons, London, 1928), and, not to repeat himself, refers the interested reader to that work.

"RUSSIAN" DIADEM OF THE EMPRESS EUGÉNIE,
WITH TWELVE HUNDRED BRILLIANTS AND FOUR
HUNDRED AND FORTY-TWO ROSE-CUT STONES
Made by Bapst, Paris, 1863

money. Gold boxes found a place in the *corbeilles* of French
princesses for presentation to various court dignitaries, and
varied in value from about 200 to 2,600 francs.   They came to
be, not unreasonably, regarded as a measure of the giver's
esteem for the recipient.   Having regard to the thousands
commonly expended it was taken as a deliberate insult when,
at the marriage of Louis XV to Maria Leszynska, the French
court presented the mother of the bride with an amber box
worth about 1,200 francs.   Even Leopold Mozart received
one worth 1,800 francs when he brought his remarkable little
son to Versailles in 1764.

When any of the Austrian Archduchesses left home to make
a foreign marriage, the Empress Maria Theresa arranged before
the bride's departure to whom gold boxes were to be distributed
en route.   The Archduchess Maria Caroline, travelling to Naples
in 1768, gave Prince Colonna "a box with a diamond lip"
worth 1800 florins, while other ladies and gentlemen had to
be content with boxes worth from 1000 to 1200 florins.   When
Marie Antoinette set out to meet her fate in 1770, her instructions ran: "Count Daun, Lord Steward of the Household in
Munich, a box worth 4000 florins, the High Steward at Munich,
one for 500 florins, the Controller of the Household, a box for 50
ducats, the Postmaster one for 100 ducats." "Small gold boxes"
are assigned to the representatives of the city of Augsburg,

253

while Baron Kagenegg of Freiburg receives another with "a diamond lip."

The French Republic did not abolish this courtly custom. During the Consulate gold boxes with the monogram RF in diamonds to the value of 5000 to 15,000 francs were used as presents to foreign diplomats. Napoleon at his coronation distributed gold boxes with his monogram in diamonds varying in value from 1,100 to 6,500 francs. When Josephine visited Germany in 1806 she gave her physician at Wiesbaden a box worth 2,100 francs, and at Frankfort-on-Main she presented gold boxes with her monogram, the most costly being worth 7,200 francs. In 1801, Cardinal Consalvi, having concluded the Concordat in Paris, received a box worth 30,000 francs from the First Consul, and the successful diplomat ordered in his will that all his boxes should be sold and the proceeds devoted to the erection of a memorial to Pope Pius VII and to the restoration of the ruined churches of Rome.

During the eighteenth century boxes were frequently objects of the collector's mania, ladies being often no less zealous than gentlemen in this matter. Maria Josepha of Saxony, dying in 1767, left valuable boxes by the dozen, among them some cut from single pieces of amethyst, a score in Meissen and Sèvres porcelain, etc. Someone counted three hundred and seventy - five gold boxes lying scattered about the suite of rooms occupied by Queen Sophia Dorothea of Prussia at Monbijou; the most valuable was worth 800 talers and was made of mother-of-pearl enclosed in gold filigree work and "richly set with brilliants." Frederick the Great, as is well known, inherited his mother's love of boxes and it was the one hobby he permitted himself. He made his own designs for the decoration of his snuff-boxes and often brought jewellers to Potsdam to work under his own eyes. Bills sent in to him for these articles vary from 50 to 12,000 talers.

In shape these boxes were most frequently quadrilateral (sometimes with rounded or blunted corners), round or oval, but no bounds were set to the maker's fancy. Boxes have come down to us shaped like clusters of grapes, vases,

portmanteaus, snails, baskets, pears, frogs, pug-dogs, lions, slippers, watches, skulls, etc. There is a box in the Ole Olsen collection shaped like a dog's head cut in amethyst with rubies for eyes. There were also trick boxes which would not open, and others which would only open by a carefully concealed spring which baffled the uninitiated. Enamelled

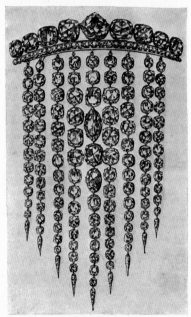

COMB OF THE EMPRESS EUGÉNIE, WITH TWO
HUNDRED AND EIGHT DIAMONDS
Made by Bapst, Paris, 1856

boxes were often decorated with pictures both within and without, the inner ones being frequently too improper for general display. Makers competed with each other in the invention of more or less cunning devices, and there were boxes with movable pictures, some of which were susceptible of as many as four variations.

Expenditure on these articles knew no limits. In the Green Vault, Dresden, is a box made of emerald matrix, and among the Wittelsbach treasures at Munich a box whose lid consists of a thirty-carat hexagonal emerald.

The uses to which these little boxes were put were almost as numerous as the forms and substances employed in their construction. During the eighteenth century the snuff-box predominated, but it was not the oldest of the sisterhood, the "bonbonnière," or comfit-box, having the prior claim. As early as 1471 King René of Sicily possessed one made of rock-crystal at his castle at Angers. From the sixteenth century onwards they were in common use among both ladies and gentlemen and were usually hung at the girdle. They were often made to look like watches, so that their wearers might at least appear to own those rare curiosities. At the market at St. Germain Henry IV brought a "bonbonnière" with the twelve signs of the zodiac engraved upon it for his natural son, little César de Vendôme. Duke François de Guise was shot by the assassin Poltrot in 1563 at the very moment of taking a sweet from his comfit-box, and twenty-five years later, when Henry III summoned the murdered duke's son to the castle at Blois where that monarch's hired assassins were already awaiting him, the messenger who delivered the treacherous summons found him filling his "bonbonnière" with candied fruits; it is unlikely that he ever ate them. Gabrielle d'Estrées, dying in 1599, left a "bonbonnière" of rock-crystal and gold enamel valued at 25 talers. Louis XIV always carried a gold "bonbonnière," as he constantly chewed aniseed to disguise the foulness of his breath. Even Napoleon never went out without a "bonbonnière" in his pocket.

Ladies also carried boxes containing cosmetics and beauty-patches. The bad taste shown by some women of our own day, who use their lip-sticks with the greatest freedom in public, had its origin in the eighteenth century. Every lady painted at that time and touched up her rouge when occasion required. For this purpose boxes were used with a mirror set inside the lid. One of Marie Antoinette's wedding presents was a gold box for rouge decorated with translucent blue enamel and worth 1,200 francs. Boxes for patches were

PLATE XVI

SNUFF-BOXES DE LUXE

From Frederick the Great's Collection
Hohenzollern Museum, Berlin

NECKLACE OF TWENTY-THREE DIAMONDS, WITH THE SMALL SANCY (34½ CARAT) AS A PENDANT; LARGE BREAST ORNAMENT IN DIAMONDS; AND TWO EARRINGS WORN BY THE EMPRESS AUGUSTA VICTORIA
Hohenzollern heirlooms

equally popular, and these too were provided with little mirrors. When the newly-wed Queen of Spain passed through France in 1714, Louis XIV sent her three gold patch-boxes for which he paid 6,000 francs. In 1747 the Crown Princess of Saxony was given four boxes for this purpose, valued at 3,880 francs. Those contained in *corbeilles* varied in price from 200 to 2,600 francs. Mme de Pompadour possessed a patch-box, enamelled and shaped like a swan, for which she paid 575 francs, and in 1757 she bought another from Lazare Duvaux for 600 francs.

Snuff-boxes were most numerous of all, because they were used by both sexes. In 1716 Lady Mary Wortley Montagu attended an entertainment for ladies at the court of the widowed Empress Amelia in Vienna, at which the young Archduchesses and their ladies shot at a mark, the first prize being a gold snuff-box. Not only elderly women and men, but quite young girls took snuff. Mme de Maintenon detested the fashion, yet despite the strictness of her rule she had to put up with seeing the ladies who attended her defiling their nostrils with snuff. It was none too easy to take a pinch with grace, and the movements involved in the whole process of opening the snuff-box, taking the pinch between two finger-tips, inhaling, closing the box and brushing the grains of snuff from the jabot were all carefully studied and practised.

As the manufacture of snuff-boxes was far in excess of the need, it was considered good form not only to have a number in use at the same time, but also to change them as frequently as possible. Mercier writes in 1781 that Parisian society used different snuff-boxes in winter and summer, and that some people carried a new one in their pockets every day. Napoleon was little addicted to snuff, yet he always carried a snuff-box and made special mention in his will of those which he still possessed in St. Helena. The first King of Bavaria loved snuff and added a number of costly snuff-boxes to the Wittelsbach heirlooms; one has on the cover a butterfly with wings of labradorite, the body being made of rubies, emeralds, sapphires, topazes and opals, set in a frame made of little plates of jasper, agate and chalcedony, the metal parts of the box being gold; another is octagonal, in silver gilt with sides of rock-crystal and eight classical cameos, knobs of carved coral at the sixteen corners and more than a thousand semi-precious stones, chrysolite, jacinth, topaz, amethyst, turquoise, garnet and emerald.

When snuff-taking ceased in good society the snuff-box was no longer an article of luxury, and was turned out by

258

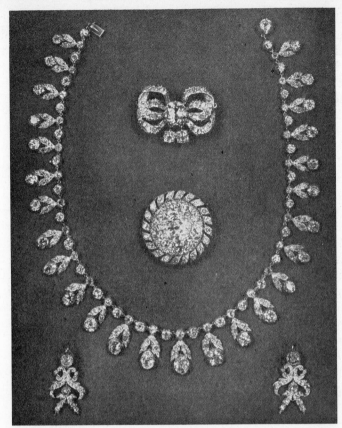

THE SO-CALLED "BRILLANTFRANSENKOLLIER," WITH EARRINGS, BUTTON AND BOW FROM NAPOLEON'S HAT, CAPTURED AT GENAPPE, 18 JUNE, 1815
Hohenzollern heirlooms

factories and workshops in common materials, horn, brass, pinchbeck, wood, earthenware, and the like. During the first half of the nineteenth century tobacco-smoking began to oust snuff-taking, and as at this period a great deal of jewelry was again being displayed upon the person the vast majority of precious eighteenth-century snuff-boxes probably found their way to the melting-pot and the gems adorning them reappeared in earrings, brooches, rings, bracelets and necklaces.

Among the many "trick" boxes which did not really serve their apparent ends we may fairly count the golden eggs which seem to have had such extraordinary popularity during the eighteenth century. One such golden egg was included in the property which the Margarvine Augusta Sybilla of Baden-Baden left at her death in 1775. On opening it a yolk of enamel appeared in which was concealed a sitting hen; the hen hid a little crown, which covered in its turn a portrait in miniature of the Margrave Louis William. This pretty toy was valued at 350 florins. A very similar specimen exists in the Green Vault, but in this case the crown, set with diamonds and pearls, surrounds a seal with a picture of a storm-tossed ship and the inscription "Constant malgré l'orage" cut upon it; the crown itself expands so that two hoops of it form a ring set with a table-cut stone which can be lifted out. Somewhat less complex, but otherwise very similar, is a specimen in the Imperial Museum, Vienna, in which the inscription on the seal is "Pour sa gloire." A great many trick boxes of all kinds were made of turned ivory, and these have come down to us in large numbers as their material did not allow of breaking up and use for other purposes.

From the sixteenth to the eighteenth century the practice of the turner's craft was very popular amongst princes of royal blood as this occupation afforded a chance of exercising their bodies which etiquette forbade in many other directions. The Emperors Rudolph II, Ferdinand III, Leopold I and Joseph II, and Electors Maurice and Augustus of Saxony, George William of Brandenburg, Maximilian I and Ferdinand of Bavaria, John William of the Palatinate and many others were passionately fond of working in ivory. In 1628 the Archduke Leopold proudly showed Philip Hainhofer his workshop and some specimens of his handiwork. All the more important collections of bygone works of art possess pieces of this kind. At the Rosenborg in Copenhagen there is a turned ivory case with a pair of compasses made by Peter the Great having a portrait of the Czar on the cover, also boxes made by Kings Frederick III, Frederick IV, and Christian VI, and a remarkable piece of work done by the Swedish general, Magnus Stenbock, during his imprisonment in Denmark in 1714, consisting of a box with a so-called "annulus Trinitatis"—a threefold ring cut in a single piece of ivory of which the several parts can be moved, but not separated from one another.   The Imperial Museum in

A LARGE BREAST ORNAMENT IN DIAMONDS AND PEARLS
Hohenzollern heirlooms

Vienna contains an ivory snuff-box shaped as a man with diamond eyes.

Similar to boxes were the "étuis" used in olden days to carry all kinds of articles for personal use.   These were extremely ornate in the eighteenth century.   Some were made to fasten to the girdle and to hold pins, sewing requisites, toothpicks, spectacles and all sorts of other small necessaries.   The toothpick has a long history, but did not become a subject of ornament till medieval times.   It was probably worn like a pendant about the neck.   When the palace at Stettin was looted on 21 June, 1574, among other articles stolen was a gold chain

worth 300 crowns "on which hangs a toothpick and an ear
spoon set with ten small turquoises." In an inventory of the
property of the Duke of Burgundy taken in 1487 there is listed
a gold toothpick set with diamonds and a single large pearl
a form of ornament which long remained in vogue. In 1660
an inventory of the property of the Archduke Leopold William
records "a gold toothpick, upon it a ring with a pointed dia
mond and a ruby in the shape of a hand." The Electoral
Prince of Brandenburg, later first King of Prussia, possessed
in 1688 two gold toothpicks, one set with a pearl, two hyacinths
and a diamond, and the other made like a claw and set with
a ruby and several diamonds. In 1715 "Amaranthes" writes
of "bediamonded ornamental pins which ladies use instead
of toothpicks." Queen Sophia Dorothea bequeathed Frederick
the Great a gold toothpick with an imitation stone set *à jour*
On the whole, however, people preferred to decorate the case
containing this indispensable implement rather than the toothpick itself. In 1534 King Francis I of France bought from
the Parisian jeweller, Regnault Danet, a gold toothpick and
ear-spoon in a case of rock-crystal and enamelled gold. In
1578 the Emperor Maximilian II bequeathed to the Archduke
Ernest a gold case and toothpick valued at 32 gulden. In
ornamental toys of this sort humour was often expressed in
the form of construction. The toothpick-case of the Electress
Kunigunde of Bavaria, wife of Maximilian Emmanuel, was in
the shape of a harlequin in dark red-stained ivory and gold.
Another, carved in amber, showed upon the inner side of the
lid a heart enclosed in a woman's breast with the inscription
" J'y resterai tant que je vivrai." A catalogue of the Imperial
Treasury, Vienna, made in 1731 mentions, besides a number of
gold toothpick-cases set with diamonds and rubies, one with an
outer case of steel, green enamelled and set with numerous
diamonds "lined, with gold inside and containing a toothpick-
case in the shape of a little blackamoor with diamonds and
rubies." The Crown Princess of Saxony received as a wedding
present a gold enamelled box for a toothpick to the value of 450
francs. Napoleon was content with one in ivory, costing about

14 francs, for his personal use, but in 1810 he gave Marie Louise a toothpick-case in chased gold for which he paid 480 francs.

Ladies used numerous little boxes for their sewing materials, pins, scissors, pocket - knives, and the like. In the Green Vault there are gold needle-cases set with precious stones in the shape of muskets, guitars, etc., and one which is a copy of the miraculous image of the Santo Bambino in the Ara Cœli church in Rome. The Ole Olsen collection contains an ivory étui with scissors, needle-case, needles and thimble in enamelled gold. Articles of this kind presented by the French Court to ladies of rank fetched fabulous prices. In 1730 the Princess of Sardinia received the gift of a gold étui set with diamonds which had cost 9,000 francs, the Queen of Spain, in 1752, a work-box in Vincennes porcelain worth 4,520 francs, the Comtesse de Provence, in 1771, a gold work-case with a chain to attach it to the waist set with 2,533 brilliants and 221 rose-cut stones, worth 28,000 francs, a sum represented by something like five thousand pounds in pre-war money.

The *corbeille* of the Princess of Saxony contained étuis for distribution varying in value from 200 to 3,000 francs.

In 1770 the Duchesse de Brissac possessed a work-box in oriental agate and gold, set with twenty brilliants, and Queen Louisa of Prussia, on her death, left a gold étui encrusted with real pearls including nineteen oriental pear-drop pearls, valued at 2,000 talers. Napoleon used a *nécessaire* of steel which he bequeathed to his uncle, Cardinal Fesch.

Though ladies certainly liked to have a pair of scissors always at hand, and, as old portraits show, carried them attached to their girdles, examples of gold scissors in gold sheaths to be seen in the Munich Treasury, and the gold scissors set with diamonds mentioned in an inventory of the Viennese regalia in 1731, were probably no more than toys and ornaments.

In our account of these exquisite little works of art we next come to the flasks and scent-bottles which took the place of the earlier "musk-apples" from the time that fluid displaced dry perfumes. The earliest known to us appear in an inventory of the goods of the Duchess Margaret, Regent of the Netherlands, who died in 1530, and were made of glass encased in a filigree of gold and silk. More expensive materials were soon employed. In 1578 the Emperor Maximilian II bequeathed to the Archduke Matthias "a gold flask of perfumed waters," valued at 82 florins. The Archduke Leopold William, whose estate was inventoried on his death in 1660, possessed "a hexagonal flask, in split agate, enclosed in gold filigree and set with turquoises," presented to him by the Empress Eleanor, besides other scent-bottles in gold filigree network set with very fine rubies and six large and numerous small pearls. The scent-bottle, however, like the snuff-box, reached its zenith of perfection in the eighteenth century. At no period was personal cleanliness less regarded, and the demand for scents was consequently imperative. The most costly materials were used in making these flasks, such as gold, silver, artificial ruby, aventurine, amalgatholith, porcelain, paste of all kinds, Wedgwood ware, amber, enamel, etc. A great variety of shapes were in vogue, including tiny bottles, boxes, eggs, bulbs, pistols, butterflies, hands, animals' heads, acorns, roses, fish, gourds, baskets, vases, urns, watches, etc., and many

264

ingenious combinations were invented. Scent-bottle-hunting-whistles were produced and a perfume flask in the Hohenzollern Museum can be expanded into a telescope. Many were made with comic intent, and it must be confessed that the "age of gallantry" had a predilection for little scent-bottles in human shape, mostly in indecorous postures, which were filled by un-screwing the head while the sprinkler was placed at the other end of the figure, either at back or front. The Rolas du Rosey collection contained numbers of such samples of wit; they might be popular at a time like the present which prides itself on concealing nothing from the light of day!

Scent-bottles formed acceptable presents to ladies of all ages, and in 1731 the fourteen-year-old Archduchess Maria Theresa received "consequent upon an *exercitium scholasticum*, the gift of a gold *eau de la Reyne* flask, set with diamonds, in a shagreen case with gold studs." Still more costly specimens are to be found in the Green Vault, Dresden, the Munich Treasury, the Court Museum, Vienna, and similar collections.

Another pretty trifle, a needlework accessory, played a considerable role as an ornament in the eighteenth century, namely the shuttle or netting-needle, in French *navette*. Then, as occasionally now, women used this dainty tool in the making of a kind of narrow lace known as netting. Mme de Genlis calls this "useless" work a symbol expressive of the good woman's detestation of total idleness. However that may be, it was a dainty, attractive amusement, excellently adapted to display lovely hands in graceful movement. Netting-needles were expensive. In 1755 Lazare Duvaux sold a gold enamelled netting-needle to the Marquise de Pompadour for 690 francs. In 1771 the Comtesse de Provence gave Mme de Beaumont a gold netting-needle, decorated with miniature paintings, worth 900 francs. The estate of the Duke of Lorraine was found to contain, on his death in 1781, seventeen netting-needles (presumably belonging to his wife) in amber, rock-crystal, gold, mother-of-pearl, agate, petrified wood, etc., all set in gold. The Electress Maria Antonia of Saxony possessed a gold netting-needle set with brilliants, which also served her

Anny Hystak
PENDANT-BROOCH IN MOONSTONES
AND DIAMONDS

as a snuff-box; on her death in 1780, she left it to the Princess Elizabeth.

Gentlemen, being practically restricted to the snuff-box, were less well off for playthings than ladies, who had snuff-box, fan, netting-needle and a dozen other toys. Moreover, the eighteenth century steadily robbed the men of personal jewelry. By the second half of that century fashion already restricted them to rings, watches and watch-chains, the latter being often worn in pairs, flaunted very conspicuously, and hung with trinkets which were intended to tinkle pleasantly; lessons in the art of making them do so were given in Paris.

About 1780 the fashion for ornate buttons received a fresh impetus; they were worn as large as five-franc pieces, affording ample scope for display of fancy. They were often adorned with miniatures, and artists of renown, such as Isabey and others, made a living in their youth by painting buttons. Between 1786 and 1795 Neubert, the court jeweller in Dresden, sold buttons made of the semi-precious stones found in Saxony, set in gold or silver; a set of a dozen in chalcedony, for example, cost 26 reichstalers.

During the last thirty years or so of the century, when Rousseau had made "sensibility" fashionable, ornaments appeared whose value consisted not in costliness of material but in sentimental associations. We find medallions and rings containing silhouettes, or little pictures of weeping-willows, altars, etc., executed as touchingly and mournfully as possible in the hair of the owner's loved ones, living or departed. In France, women and girls of the working classes wore little crosses on narrow ribbons about their necks, called "Saint-Esprits": they became an indispensable part of dress, and the famous soubrette, Mme Favart, did not forget the "Saint-

266

Esprit" which lent the last touch of realism to the peasant costume she wore on the stage. Then, as ever, much jewelry was required for a lady's full-dress toilet. The V-shaped openings of the tightly-laced bodices were often so richly adorned with precious stones that they appeared one large orna-

Anny Hystak

RING-BROOCH IN GOLD WITH DIAMONDS AND PEARLS

ment. Maria Theresa had the famous "*Esclavage*" made for this purpose from the largest and finest stones among the Habsburg heirlooms. Everyone will remember the famous "necklace affair" in France. A "collier" of brilliants, set by the jewellers Boehmer and Bassange for Marie Antoinette, who, however, rejected it as too expensive, was stolen from the firm by a female swindler who called herself the Comtesse de Lamotte Valois and who sold the article in London. Proceedings indiscreetly instituted by the French Government against persons, some innocent and some guilty, concerned in this matter, gravely compromised the Queen, and the "affair of the necklace" did much to precipitate the catastrophe which soon afterwards broke over France and the whole world.

The Revolution, and the financial disasters which invariably accompany such upheavals in the state, robbed the gentlemen of their silver shoe-buckles, which had to be sacrificed on the altar of patriotism. They were replaced by cut-steel buckles and about the end of the century these appeared also in England which was also passing through a series of financial crises and needed all the precious metal it could lay hands on. When the Terror was over and a new society began to revel in new-found riches, jewelry reappeared and that, answering to the tastes of the *nouveaux riches*, in superabundance. Ladies adopted what they believed to be classical modes and wore bracelets and anklets, rings on fingers and toes, chains wound six- and seven-fold about the neck, earrings with triple drops, combs, diadems, ornamental pins, etc. The Empire period encouraged these parvenu modes, for the mass of jewelry looted and sent home by French commanders from all parts of the world cried out for display. Wealth flowed to the Napoleonic court. Mme Duroc possessed a hundred thousand talers' worth of diamonds, Mme Ney a hundred thousand francs' worth, the wives of Maret and Savary each owned fifty thousand francs' worth. At a fancy-dress ball in the Tuileries, when a procession of Peruvians to the Temple of the Sun was represented, jewelry worn by the ladies present was valued at twenty million francs.

Much, however, escaped the French freebooters. In addition to three hundred other costly ornaments Countess Potocka possessed a hundred and forty-four rings, and the Esterhazy heirlooms were worth seven million gulden. The state dress of a Hungarian grandee, sewn all over with pearls, was estimated to be worth four million gulden and cost eight thousand gulden to repair after each occasion of wearing. Countess Voss, Mistress of the Robes at the Prussian Court, tells us in her diary that for long she saw no jewels there, but Queen Louisa managed to preserve her own private jewels through the worst days and when she died in July, 1810, left eight hundred and thirty-seven pearls, of which a hundred and thirty very large ones were worth 6,500 talers. She possessed an "esclavage" in brilliants worth 10,000 talers and an aigrette worth 20,000 talers. The value of her twenty-eight personal ornaments amounted to 94,913 talers. Queen Louisa was particularly fond of aquamarines and amethysts, which in her time were reckoned as precious stones though shortly afterwards large finds of them in the Ural mountains and Brazil reduced them to the category of semi-precious stones.

The women and girls of Prussia sacrificed what little the French had left them to save their ruined country and took to wearing iron ornaments, polished or black, made by Berlin manufacturers in light and tasteful designs. Crosses, chains, medallions, rings, combs and bracelets in iron, often brightened by a modest addition of gold, kept their popularity in Prussia till the eighteen-thirties. The high nobility, of course, had no need to resort to the iron ornaments of humbler patriots, and when they organised a knightly quadrille at the Hofburg in Vienna during the Congress, the ladies taking part carried some thirty million francs' worth of jewels on their persons, Princess Esterhazy alone wearing six millions' worth.

Napoleon had the great French crown diamonds set in his hat and sword-hilt. When he was obliged to abandon his coach to avoid capture on his flight from the field of Waterloo, the vehicle and all its contents fell into the hands of Prussian troops. In it the fusiliers of the Fifteenth Foot found the Corsican's hat-buckle, ornamented with twenty-two immense solitaires and a hundred and twenty-one small brilliants; its value was estimated at twenty thousand talers. The regiment sent it to King Frederick William III, who ordered it to be deposited with the crown jewels. At the same time the "Sancy" fell into Prussian hands; this was one of the finest stones in the former French crown jewels, and though its weight in the process of cutting had been reduced from the original four hundred and ten carats to fifty-three carats, despite this loss it remained a most magnificent gem.

The so-called "classical" modes of the Revolution and the Empire revived a taste for real antiques, especially for the cameo. Marshals of the French armies sent the valuable collections of Roman princes to Paris, where the Empress Josephine, heedlessly extravagant, gave away the most precious pieces of antique jewelry to her ladies by the handful. All contemporary portraits show the fair sitters with necklaces, diadems and bracelets set with cameos. The crown with which Napoleon crowned himself King of Italy was set, it is true, with paste instead of real stones, but he was less economical where his wife was concerned and requisitioned eighty-two of the best antique cameos from the national collections which the jeweller Nitot set with two thousand two hundred and seventy-five pearls to make a diadem, comb, necklace, pair of earrings and pair of bracelets for Josephine, who found them magnificent, but too heavy to wear. Queen Louisa of Prussia also loved cameo jewelry. In 1802 Grassi painted her portrait displaying a diadem adorned with a portrait cameo of Frederick William III set in diamonds. The Empress Augusta left the Grand Duchess Maria Paulovna's wonderful diamond-set cameo ornaments to the Prussian crown jewels; they were valued at 30,000 marks.

These cameos were so eagerly sought that the supply of genuine stones was insufficient to meet the demand and the dealers satisfied their customers with shell cameos. It is easier and quicker to work in shell than in the harder and more brittle substance of stone. The varying colour of this material enables the artist to obtain almost the effects of a painting, it offers larger surfaces and is infinitely cheaper. In the course of the nineteenth century the shell cameo completely supplanted the true cameo cut in stone (*pietra dura*). From time to time fashion favoured extravagantly large ones. Really beautiful garlanded profiles could be bought in Naples at one time for a few lire.

In the Victorian age, the golden age of bourgeois society, fashion deprived the male sex of the right to wear jewelry, other than watch-chain, tie-pin and ring, but at the same time heaped the woman with jewels. In the twenties a fashionable woman would wear at one and the same time, diadem, comb, and jewelled pins in the hair, a necklace and a long fine gold chain about the neck, bracelets over her sleeves, rings outside her gloves, long earrings, a brooch in her bodice and a clasp at her belt, and if in addition she carried a gold or silver bouquet-holder and a fan set with diamonds she displayed no more ornament than the mode had established as indispensable. Contrasts were deliberately emphasised between dress and jewelry, and in 1821 the beautiful Mme Gros-Davillier wore at a ball in Paris a simple white tulle dress and a fortune in diamonds. Jewelry worn by the Baroness Rothschild in 1842 at a ball given by the Duke of Orleans was judged to be worth one and half million francs. In 1836 Mme Schickler lost a single pearl worth twenty-five thousand francs at a ball at the Tuileries.

In the thirties "medieval" jewelry was the *dernier cri* in Paris. There was no question of imitations of genuine period pieces but rather, as with the so-called "Gothic" furniture of that epoch, of reconstructions by means of the free use of architectural forms copied from the old cathedrals. Despite these stylistic distortions, however, certain jewellers such as Vever, Froment-Meurice, Bapst, Petiteau and Falize produced some very exquisite work.

For several decades ladies went with neck and arms uncovered, a fashion which urgently demanded jewelry to complete its effect. It was worn both by day and in the evening and according to prevailing taste and fashion could not be overdone. Amber, rock-crystal, Venetian glass beads, settings of hair and Roman pearls were considered suitable for day wear. After the marriage of a Princess of the Two Sicilies to the Duc d'Aumale in 1845 coral became once more fashionable. Gay coloured effects in enamel were very popular, bracelets and brooches were made in the form of wide bows, and ornaments in general could hardly be too large or too staring. It was considered indispensable to carry several wide bracelets on the arm at once, while earrings became very long and elaborate in construction and brooches and medallions became veritable placards. For the evening toilet precious stones were worn when possible. The Empress Eugénie had a border made for a ball dress into which were worked the French crown jewels; it was made of rubies, emeralds, sapphires, turquoises, hyacinths, topazes and garnets blended together with many hundreds of diamonds. Bapst, Krammer and Lemonnier set some marvellous jewels for the beautiful Spaniard, among them the famous vine-leaf jewel, whose garlands were made of more than three thousand brilliants, a comb of two hundred and eight large brilliants, a belt of pearls, sapphires, rubies and emeralds blended together with two thousand four hundred brilliants, diadems and numerous other ornaments, whose splendour was, nevertheless, further enhanced by the fact that they were worn by the most beautiful woman in the world.

Ornaments had to be worn in profusion to make any sort

of show. At her coronation at Königsberg on 18 August, 1861, Queen Augusta of Prussia wore the sixty-four largest brilliants of the crown upon her corsage, a diamond necklace containing the "Sancy" and two ropes of seventy-one matched pearls, including seven large pear-shaped pearls. While still but Crown Princess of Prussia the future Empress possessed a famous set of emeralds which after her death was by her own wish allocated to the crown jewels and which was estimated to be worth 150,000 marks, the diadem to match being valued

Rothmüller

PENDANT IN GOLD WITH AMETHYSTS,
PEARLS AND CHRYSOLITE

Rothmüller

PENDANT IN GOLD, SILVER,
OPALS, RUBIES AND PEARLS

at 20,000 marks. In 1862 Frau von Bismarck saw the Czarina at St. Petersburg wearing diamonds worth fifteen million roubles. In 1869 the Duchesse de Mouchy wore two millions' worth of diamonds at a ball, while the great courtesans of the Parisian *demi-monde*, Léonide Leblanc, Thérèse Lachmann, Élise Musard, Cora Pearl and the rest, completely eclipsed even the great ladies of the *monde*.

The wholesale manufacture of jewelry which sprang up in the nineteenth century had disastrous effects upon taste and style. Gold, pressed to the thinness of paper and made up in feeble designs, is characteristic of machine-made ornaments for many decades. Some improvement set in when people began to return to the ancient models, but mass production, with its technical limitations and enslavement to the machine, permitted no real progress. In this matter the individual goldsmith is wanted, producing sound workmanship and expressing his individual taste. There were very promising signs of a revival before the war. Since about 1895 craftsmen like R. Lalique have shown a possible way to a renaissance of the jeweller's art. Feeling for material, for the values of colour and brilliance, is more necessary than a one-sided predilection for size and number of gems to be employed in ornament. But to get this a public with taste and education is necessary. Where are we to look for one?

MADE AT THE
TEMPLE PRESS
LETCHWORTH
GREAT BRITAIN